SPARTANBURG

Portrait of the Good Life

▲ JAMES HUFF

SPARTANBURG

Portrait of the Good Life

by Scott Gould
and Mark Olencki

Corporate Profiles by
Peggy O'Neal

Art Direction by
Brian Groppe

Produced in Cooperation
with the Spartanburg Area
Chamber of Commerce

T O W E R Y   P U B L I S H I N G ,   I N C .

Library of Congress Cataloging-in-Publication Data

Gould, Scott, 1959-
    Spartanburg : portrait of the good life / by Scott Gould and Mark
Olencki ; corporate profiles by Peggy O'Neal; art director, Brian
Groppe.
        p.   cm.— (Urban tapestry series)
    "Produced in cooperation with the Spartanburg Area Chamber of
Commerce."
    Includes index.
    ISBN 1-881096-04-1: $39.50
    1. Spartanburg (S.C.)—Civilization. 2. Spartanburg (S.C.)—
Pictorial works. 3. Spartanburg (S.C.)—Industries. I. Olencki,
Mark, 1953-   . II. O'Neal, Peggy, 1953-   . III. Groppe, Brian.
IV. Title.   V. Series.
F279.S7G68   1993
975.7'29—dc20   93-44112
                                                                              CIP

TOWERY Publishing, Inc.
1835 Union Avenue, Suite 142
Memphis, TN 38104

Publisher:	J. Robert Towery
Editorial Directors:	Patricia M. Towery
	David Dawson
Senior Editors:	Michael C. James
	Ken Woodmansee
Articles Editor:	Allison Jones Simonton
Assistant Art Director:	Anne Castrodale
Technical Director:	William H. Towery
Copy Editor:	Stinson Liles

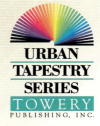

URBAN
TAPESTRY
SERIES
TOWERY
PUBLISHING, INC.

Contents

I HAVE A CONFESSION. THE FIRST TIME I SAW SPARTANBURG, IT FOOLED ME. I WAS DRIVING through town, headed for the campus of Wofford College. A friend had told me Wofford was the best kept academic secret south of Duke University, so I thought I'd check it out and see if I might want to attend school there. I'll admit, I was younger then, maybe too naive to notice the finer points of things. But my earliest recollection of Spartanburg is the color brown. Just brown, everywhere I looked.

The sky—or rather the low-lying clouds—had sucked up the sun and thrown a burlap glow on the city's streets. The folks who were out, braving the chilly breeze, wore brown overcoats. The fallen leaves that had somehow escaped the rake were...well, you get the point.

But like I said, I was young. Back then, my rash conclusions were as common as raindrops on a cloudy day. The next morning, the wind had died down, the sun was out in all its glory, and—much to my surprise—so was Spartanburg. I can't begin to tell you how wrong I'd been about the city.

Since that day over 15 years ago, I've been a proud fan of Spartanburg. Not a braying, loud-mouthed spectator, but rather a more subtle, adopted son who has watched the city grow—correctly and on its own terms—into a gathering spot for business visionaries, entrepreneurs, artists, teachers, farmers, shift workers, modern immigrants...anybody who wants to snag a fair share of the good life.

You see, Spartanburg isn't a boom-and-bust city like those that have had their day in the sun and are now first cousins to a ghost town. No, Spartanburg has drawn stamina and strength from its mill village past and used that hard-earned grit and backbone to build the kind of community where seventh-generation native sons can share an iced tea with the newest German family on the block.

It's the kind of place that *juxtaposes* the best that people have to offer. I suppose the "J" word is just a fancy way of saying that there's a little something here for everybody, and it's all worth sampling. A perfect example is Renato's, an elegant Italian restaurant whose owner actually drives to Chicago once a month or so for his favorite cheeses. He's the only one he trusts to pick them out.

Down the street a couple of blocks is the Nu-Way Lounge. It's a little hole-in-the-wall pub run by a guy named Bubba who wears a 24-hour-a-day smile and holds the keys to one of the last great jukeboxes in the South—a tune mecca that blasts everything from Judy Garland to Jimi Hendrix.

Bubba or Renato. Buddy Holly or Caruso. French fries or green-lipped mussels in garlic butter. Again, if you're going to understand Spartanburg, you've got to understand the "J" word. It's what keeps the place lively.

Spartanburg's location in the northwest corner of South Carolina puts it within easy reach of the area's great recreational opportunities. The beautiful Carolina beaches are only a few hours distance, and the Blue Ridge Mountains, worn smooth by the centuries, are just close enough to take your breath away at the end of the day.

Spartanburg has long been appreciative of fine dining as well as down-home cooking. As the population of the metropolitan area has passed the 225,000 mark, occasions to sample special dishes from around the world have increased tenfold. Mandarin, Mexican, Viennese, Japanese, and Indian restaurants have opened their doors alongside those that offer the best in traditional Southern fare. And the folks in Spartanburg are, as they say, just eating it up. Pictured here is a little bit of Italy at Renato's downtown.

I DON'T WANT TO FIXATE ON FOOD, but while we're on the subject, I have this friend who says the best way to find out about Spartanburg is to eat your way from one city limit sign to the other. If you do, no doubt you'll spend time at The Beacon, one of the country's largest drive-ins, and a place once profiled by Charles Kuralt. At The Beacon, you'd better know what you want when you get in line. Indecision is treated as a sin, but a healthy appetite isn't. Just to be safe, order the onion rings that melt like butter in your mouth.

Indeed, Spartanburg offers variety. Take your taste buds on a whirl at the India Palace restaurant—on the bottom floor of the Howard Johnson's—where the chef just sort of chuckles when a customer orders something spicy. Nearby, at the Piedmont Cafe, patrons can slide in front of a thick steak in the very chair where Elvis once sat in his younger, thinner days.

Truly, we celebrate Spartanburg's culinary resources. Dining is one of the ways people come together on familiar ground—it's where they talk, conduct business, and discuss a common vision

for the future.

Another way the folks in Spartanburg come together is through their love of the arts. The Spartanburg Arts Council is as strong and vocal an advocacy group as you'll find anywhere. They love to discover new artists or adopt established ones, then support them to the hilt with exhibitions, juried shows, or anything else that places local art in front of the eyes of the people.

You'll also find a wonderfully accomplished selection of theatre companies in town. For example, the Spartanburg Little Theatre has been dubbed the "best amateur theatre in the South," while the

Youth Theatre is South Carolina's oldest, full-scale children's theatre. Different Stages, Inc. performs summer theatre at the Arts Center, and the Spartanburg Repertory Theatre has been satisfying musical theatre and opera buffs since 1987.

Thespians aren't the only artists on stage in Spartanburg. The Ballet Guild and the Spartanburg Civic Ballet serve a growing dance community with a number of productions and workshops, and host national and international touring companies. In addition, for over a century, the Music Foundation of Spartanburg has showcased world-renowned performers such as Van Cliburn, Beverly Sills, and the Bolshoi Symphony Orchestra at Converse College's Twichell Auditorium.

The creative spirit is alive and well in Spartanburg. However, this spirit doesn't always manifest itself on canvas or under the floodlights. Some of the city's finest craftspeople work with tulip buds and pine mulch. Gardening, you see, is practiced here with a unique passion. Naturally, the best evidence is on display each spring in neighborhoods like Converse Heights, with its well-groomed, almost classic

MARK OLENCKI

lines, or Hampton Heights, where sprawling Victorian homes are being refurbished on every block.

In most neighborhoods, you'll find that spring is not for those whose senses are easily overloaded. Between the azaleas and dogwoods and fresh-cut lawns and the Spring Fling downtown, there are sights and smells vivid enough to last year-round. Spring, however, doesn't spite the other three seasons—they possess their own charms. Summers are hot, but the breezes that spill out of the nearby Blue Ridge Mountains keep the air moving with a welcome regularity. (A century-and-a-half ago, folks came here from the East Coast to spend their summers.) In the fall, there's always that one weekend when the leaves reinvent the color spectrum and make even the crustiest curmudgeon gawk at the display. And winters? They are short and crisp, and usually provide a couple of snowfalls which make some folks pull out their sleds, while others pull out the calendar and start the countdown to spring.

No matter what the season, Spartanburg is constantly rubbing shoulders with Moth-er Nature. A 15-minute drive in any direction will put you in her midst. The Tyger River is to the west, and sparkling Lake Bowen to the north. Farther north are the foothills of the Blue Ridge Mountains. To the east, peach orchards

MARK OLENCKI

and sprawling farmlands dot the rolling landscape.

Sounds bucolic, you might think. Well, don't be mistaken. Spartanburg is an aggressive, modern city driven by a vision of continual prosperity. Just head out I-85 or drive into the heart of town; then stick your ear to the ground and hear the rumble of growth and new development. It's hard to tell where the sound is the loudest.

THROUGHOUT SPARTANBURG County, you'll find an influx of new businesses and industries that would make any chamber of commerce bust its buttons with pride. For example, Bavarian Motor Works Manufacturing (BMW) and Helima Helvetion— two German companies—have built operations in Spartanburg, as have Dare Foods from Canada and Trimite Powders from Great Britain. And right in the middle of town, there's the Flagstar tower—headquarters for the parent company of Denny's, Quincy's, Canteen, and the largest franchiser of Hardee's restaurants. It's little wonder that Spartanburg has led the state in the number of new jobs created during seven of the past eight years.

Spartanburg's economic past is anchored in the textile mill villages that made up most of Upstate South Carolina. That anchor is still holding firm with the rise of Milliken & Company, an international corporation which conducts more than 70 percent of textile research in the United States. However, Spartanburg, to its credit, has diversified its industrial base to the point that you

Calling The Beacon just a drive-in is like calling the Mona Lisa a doodle. It's an institution, a legend, and an irreplaceable part of Spartanburg's culture. By the way, they have the best onion rings in this hemisphere.

The Spartanburg skyline is punctuated by steeples. Keep your ears open on Sunday mornings, and you'll hear the sounds of bells on the breeze. More than 200 churches representing 30 denominations instill a strong sense of community through their ministries, whether those programs are day care centers or "Mobile Meals" for the elderly and underprivileged.

almost need a scorecard to keep up with who's moving in, what services they offer, and which country they came from.

To get a feel for this industrial and business boom, stop by the Spartanburg Area Chamber of Commerce and notice the 13 international flags waving high above. Each one stands for the home country of a company doing business in Spartanburg County. By the way, that total is now up to 83 international companies, including names like adidas America, Inc., and Hoechst Celanese. The influx of companies has given Spartanburg County the highest per-capita diversified foreign investment in the United States. Couple this with the "native" industries, like Spartan Mills, and you've got the making of a strong economic base that keeps unemployment relatively low and recession at bay.

Next, take a drive along I-85. You'll notice the mixture of industries from around the globe with those companies that have been here for generations, manufacturing everything from radiator tubing to cotton cleaning machines. For instance, Packard Electric and Lear Seating have recently put down roots in the rapidly ex-

panding I-85/Highway 290 corridor. Lured by the presence of BMW, these companies will manufacture parts for the German automaker.

However, it's longtimers like Hoechst Celanese, Milliken, Spartanburg Steel,

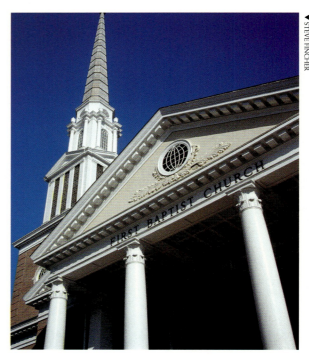

and Beverage Air that anchor the industrial boom along I-85 and give it credibility as an intelligent location to set up business. They've been here for years. They've been highly successful. And they've set a precedent for others to follow.

When you're on I-85, you're on an industrial corridor that runs from Charlotte to Atlanta, and Spartanburg is fortunate to be located roughly in the middle of that stretch. This geographical

stroke of luck makes Spartanburg attractive to firms looking to relocate or expand in the Sunbelt. Great location, nice weather, a work force backed by a solid technical education system, an unmatched quality of life, an international airport, a pro-business climate...It's no surprise that over $600 million of capital investment created 3,441 new jobs in Spartanburg in 1992— both record-breaking numbers. Consequently, when new business comes calling, Spartanburg gets on the short list. Just ask BMW.

The company had a whole continent to choose from, and they picked Spartanburg. Their only North American facility is located just outside of the city, adjacent to the Greenville-Spartanburg Airport. With the arrival of BMW, Spartanburg and neighboring Greenville have seen a number of ancillary firms flock to the Upstate to service the German carmaker. And you can bet that still more will begin springing up along the interstate.

STEVE FINCHER

I DON'T KNOW WHERE YOU SPEND YOUR SUNDAY MORNINGS. AND I'M NOT SURE OF YOUR opinion regarding the ivory towers of academia, but I can say this without blinking: Religion and education are as much a part of Spartanburg's identity as the people who live here, and if either were to be taken away, the city would crumble into a pile of bricks and mortar. ◆ This isn't a new idea. Nor is it an original one. It's simply an unescapable conclusion. Spartanburg's history is deeply rooted in its religious heritage.

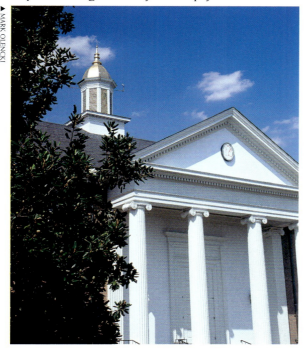

▶ MARK OLENCKI

The pioneer folk who settled the area and staked out elbow room in the shadows of the mountains felt that this was, indeed, God's country. And some- how, the good Lord reserved this peaceful place in their names. That feeling still per- petuates today, as the faithful of all denomi- nations will attest.

While religion stands as an important part of the city's past— and, no doubt, part of our future—so does the emphasis on col- lege life. But make no mistake about it: Spartanburg is *not* your typical college town. Each school is blended into the community so naturally that when the students leave for summer or holidays, it's not a shock to the city. In other towns, the college or univer- sity swells the population and sustains local businesses from September to June. Not so in

Spartanburg, where four small colleges call the city home: Wofford, Converse, the Uni- versity of South Carolina at Spartanburg, and Spartanburg Methodist.

The University of South Carolina at Spartanburg

(USCS), located on the outskirts of town, is the youngest of the local institutions. USCS is one of the stars in the large South Carolina Uni- versity system, and it has grown consis- tently in reputation and size since its doors opened in 1967.

Likewise for Spartanburg Meth- odist College (SMC). Founded in 1911, SMC has been ac- knowledged nation- ally as one of the country's finest two- year institutions.

But smack in the middle of downtown, you'll find the foundation for Spartanburg's educational tradition. Wofford and Converse—a couple of post-

Don't make the mistake of calling the University of South Carolina at Spartanburg an "extension" school or a "satellite" campus. This rapidly growing, 27-year-old university has carved out quite an identity all its own. About 5,000 undergraduate and graduate stu- dents commute to the 247-acre campus to enjoy its small classes and personalized instruction. The Spartanburg community regularly takes advantage of university art exhibits, concerts, and lectures, as well as theatre productions by the Shoestring Players.

Converse College, which celebrated its centennial in 1989, has gained a national reputation for its School of Music, not to mention its rose garden. The four-year women's college has been ranked one of the top 10 liberal arts colleges in the South by *U.S. News & World Report* since 1989.

You might hear a saying around campus: "There's the right way, the wrong way, and the Wofford Way." And for hundreds of alumni and students, the Wofford Way is the only way they'd choose. They aren't the only ones with a high opinion of the college. *U.S. News & World Report* ranked Wofford the number one liberal arts college in the South in 1990 and 1991.

age-stamp sized, private colleges—are known nationwide for their high standards and graduates who are well-versed in the liberal arts.

Converse College admitted its first class in 1889, and it remains a school for women which is recognized for its music and arts programs. Converse is rich in tradition, which is to say that if you walk across the manicured campus, among the oaks and comfortably aged buildings, you can feel its history surrounding you. Even Converse's newest structures, like the Milliken Art Building, blend unobtrusively with the rest of the turn-of-the-century architecture.

But buildings can't talk. Neither can shade trees. They can't tell the effect Converse has on the lives of the young women who have called it home for four years. Face to face with alumnae and students— that's the only way to really hear about the Converse experience. Funny thing is, they all tend to say the same thing...they wouldn't trade their time at Converse for anything in the world.

A few blocks from Converse is Wofford College. It's a small place, centered around the twin-spired Old Main Building, and home to fewer students than fill a lot of high schools. But for hundreds and hundreds of alums (myself included), Wofford occupies a huge chunk of our memory. It's the place where we arrived after first leaving home. It's the place where we came eye-to-eye with a professor who filled our imaginations with new ideas. The school is, ulti-

STEVEN STINSON

MARK OLENCKI

mately, the place that changed not just how we thought, but how we lived. And it's also how we came to know Spartanburg.

Like Converse, Wofford is unabashedly proud of its liberal arts curriculum—its ability to stand science and religion and philosophy and literature side by side, and make them understandable together. Wofford has its share of traditions, too, most of which are turned on their ears each year when bright students meet innovative instructors—a mix that results in educational fireworks. Students actually come to know their instructors. Relationships develop that last long beyond graduation. You see, Wofford has no cattle-call classes attended by 200 social security numbers. There are real people on both sides of the desk. No anonymity, because there's no crowd to hide in. Some might call this quaint. Most who experience it call it the only way to get an education.

FUNNY THING IS, WHEN I THINK OF SPARTANBURG, I DON'T DWELL ON THE BUILDINGS OR the restaurants or the water towers or the azaleas in Converse Heights. I only see faces. Good faces. Smiles shining with character. Bright eyes. Because (and you can slap my wrist for using the cliche), people make the place. Without the kind of folks you have here, Spartanburg is just another dot along the interstate. ♦ I think about the way the kids can barely sit still when they ride the miniature train in Cleveland Park, grinning

grins that push their ears apart. I think about Archie, who used to sweep the old Andrews Field House and tell stories about growing up on Mill Hill. Or Mister Roy, who gave out towels at the YMCA and could hit a three-rail combination that would send a pool shark into retirement.

And there's Will Fort who opened Main Street Books. In this day and age it's hard to imagine anyone opening a "real" bookstore miles from the nearest shopping mall. But Fort did, and with his appreciation for readers and writers, he is attracting crowds through his door regularly.

Of course, there are others that have been around forever, it seems. Like the salesmen at Price's Mens Store, who for years have helped gentlemen put together their wardrobes. And the regulars at

▲ MARK OLENCKI

▲ MARK OLENCKI

the Skillet Restaurant who use breakfast as an excuse to discuss how the Spartanburg Phillies did the night before at Duncan Park.

They're still here. The good folks, like J.C., who barks orders from behind the

counter at The Beacon. The sharp-eyed cook who tosses pizza dough at Patelli's. And the ironic thing is that most of the best people, you'll never meet. They might wave from a front porch or hold the post office door open for you. They might give you directions if you get turned around on some farm-to-market road. They make up a kind of human security blanket, something you can wrap yourself in when you wonder how someone could actually live somewhere else.

This is where hope lives, with the people because in the end, it's the folks who live here who give Spartanburg its spirit, and who make it possible for everyone—the newcomers and natives alike—to experience the good life.

Amid the city's booming economy, the arrival of major international corporations, and the advances of technology, the people of Spartanburg still rely on really important things...like the strength of family.

The Piedmont Cafe has some of the best steaks in town and some of the Upstate's finest conversationalists standing by with the local lowdown. The smiles are no charge.

JOHN GILLESPIE

Spartanburg is, above all, a grand mixture
of tastes and attitudes—a juxtaposition of
nostalgia and progress. This combination
gives the city a unique charm that's rare
these days.

The new and the old. The future and the past. They come together comfortably up and down Main Street, Spartanburg.

The methods of building construction have certainly changed; however, the Upstate area of South Carolina has been attracting settlers since the 1700s. Walnut Grove Plantation, built on a land grant from King George III, gives a real feel for the lifestyle of the Charles Moore family, which included Spartanburg County's first doctor and a Revolutionary War heroine. Thirteen areas of Spartanburg County have been placed on the National Register of Historic Places.

▼ MARK OLENCKI

Although more than 80 international companies have offices and/or manufacturing sites in Spartanburg County, the groundbreaking in 1992 for BMW's only North American manufacturing plant created the kind of excitement rarely seen in the Upstate.

▼ ROBERT GREGORY

Jerry Richardson (center), chairman and CEO of Flagstar Companies, Inc., a billion-dollar restaurant operations and food vending business headquartered in downtown Spartanburg, is owner of one of the National Football League's newest franchises. His six-and-a-half year effort is credited with landing the team, the Carolina Panthers.

Though Roger Milliken, head of the renowned textile and research company, Milliken & Company, keeps a hectic schedule, he still finds time to pull a "tie exchange" with a good friend. Speaking of exchanges, executives of Menzel, Inc., manufacturers of machinery for the textile industry, stand beside two sections of the Berlin Wall that are kept on display outside their corporate offices.

When completed in 1990, the headquarters for Flagstar Companies, Inc. was the tallest building in Spartanburg. Its appearance on the former site of the historic Franklin Hotel signaled a rebirth of the downtown area.

The architectural aesthetic of Spartanburg is constantly evolving, thanks to buildings like Evangel Cathedral that capture the innovative spirit of the city.

▲ MARK OLENCKI

▲ MARK OLENCKI

Spartanburg's skyline seems to have a different look each day, given all the development of the past decade. Sometimes it's a man-made alteration, like the demolition of a downtown hotel. Sometimes Mother Nature has a hand in things.

Spartanburg's broad industrial base and nationally recognized worker training programs combine to help keep the unemployment rate well below state and national averages.

There's a charm to Spartanburg that comes about through an almost effortless blending of different styles and sensibilities, evident not only in the diversity of the people, but also in the very architecture of the city.

Whether it's sprucing up an historic building downtown or repainting one of Spartanburg's famous twin water towers, it's worth the effort to keep the city gleaming.

The textile industry, Spartanburg's economic mainstay for well over a century, has made technological leaps and bounds in the past few years, such as automated yarn spinning. Since the 1950s, however, there has been a broadening of the city's business base, with new industries—such as manufacturers of aluminum tubing, power transmissions, and gear components—moving into the area at a record pace.

A highly skilled and motivated work force, an excellent quality of life, a decidedly pro-business climate—it's a combination that's been attracting companies from around the world. As a matter of fact, Spartanburg County has the highest per capita diversified foreign investment in the United States.

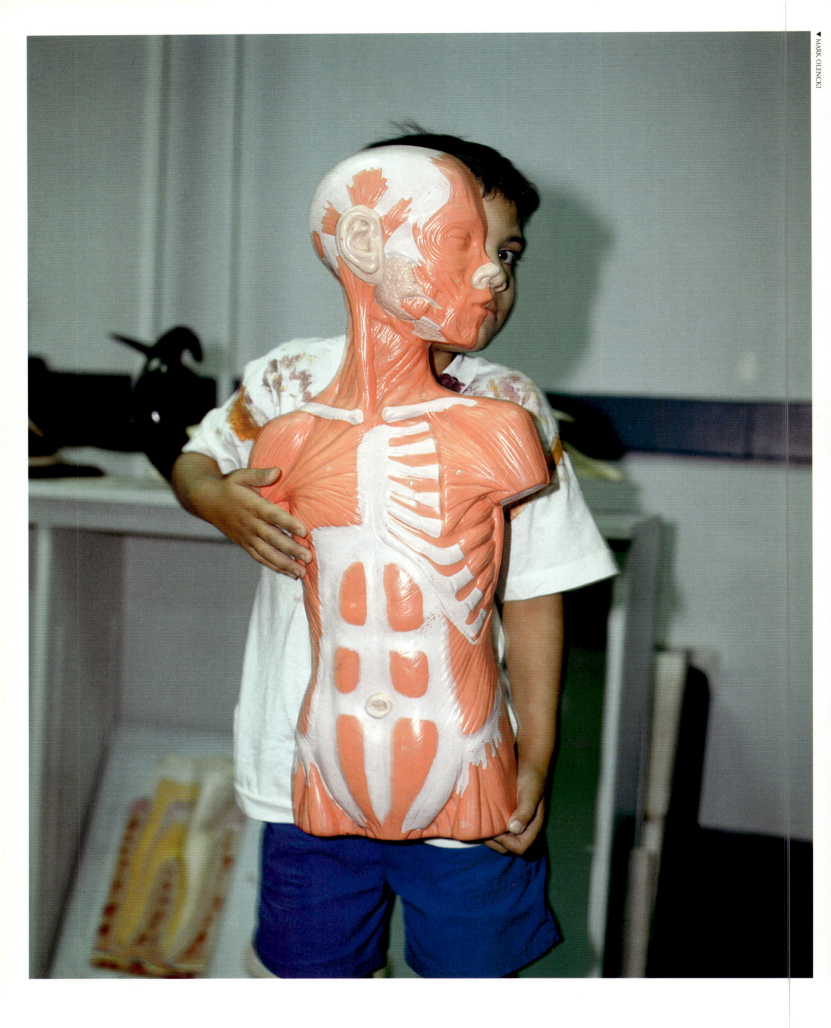

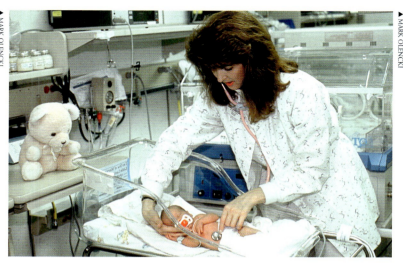

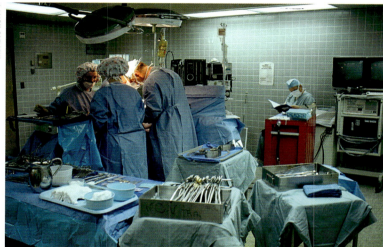

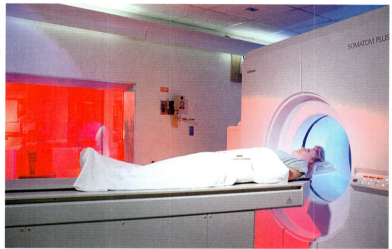

The health care market in Spartanburg is one of the most competitive in the state. Yet the competition has been healthy for consumers, creating an extremely high level of quality care. The county's four hospitals, as well as numerous clinics and private practices, provide state-of-the-art treatment in many areas of specialty, including neonatal care, cancer and heart disease, sleep disorders, trauma, and physical rehabilitation.

Folks are moving to Spartanburg and staying to carve out careers and raise their families. A walk through any neighborhood lets you know that the city's future is in good (though sometimes messy) hands.

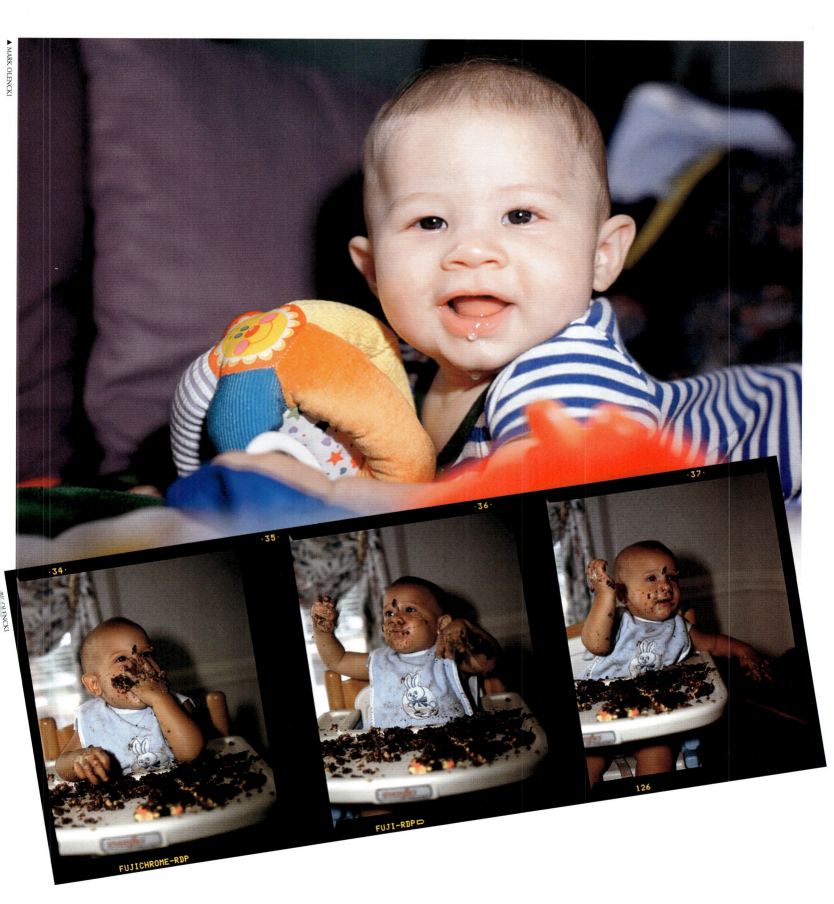

FUJICHROME-RDP

FUJI-RDP

·34· ·35· ·36· ·37·

126

Spartanburg's neighborhoods are a pretty good reflection of its people: diverse, individualistic, proud . . . the kinds of places people like to call home.

If you really want to know Spartanburg,
forget about industry and economics and
demographics. Just look at the faces.
You'll see the city's bright future smiling
back at you.

Spartanburg has its heart in the right place. People here aren't afraid to pass the hat for a good cause or hit the street to make sure the new church building has enough bricks and mortar.

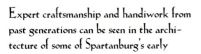

Expert craftsmanship and handiwork from past generations can be seen in the architecture of some of Spartanburg's early church buildings, like First Presbyterian (above) and the Church of the Advent Episcopal (opposite).

JOHN GEDDES
BORN IN HUNTLY
ABERDEEN SHIRE
SCOTLAND
1820-1894.

AT REST

Spartanburg features a wonderful mixture of retail establishments and specialty stores, such as Shades of the Past Antiques and The Spice of Life gourmet shop and restaurant.

Book lovers are always welcome to stay
awhile at the comfortable, well-stocked
Main St. Books. However, Spartanburg's
preeminent lover of books is found at the
Wofford College library. He's Herbert
Hucks (opposite), Archivist Emeritus
and a mainstay at the college since 1946.

There's no shortage of places to pursue one of Spartanburg's favorite pastimes— getting together with friends. There's a wide range of ambience and interiors— from banquettes to pub stools—but many people are drawn to the Elvis Chair, where the King himself sat in his "Tender" years.

In Spartanburg, the personalities behind
the menus are just as interesting as the fare.

Every fall, you can count on a couple of things—beautiful leaves and the annual International Festival. You get the opportunity to sample cultural and culinary offerings representing dozens of countries, all under one roof. In addition to being a great get-together, the festival serves as a reminder of Spartanburg's diverse ethnic character.

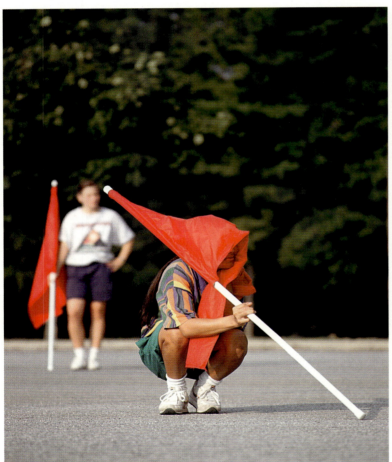

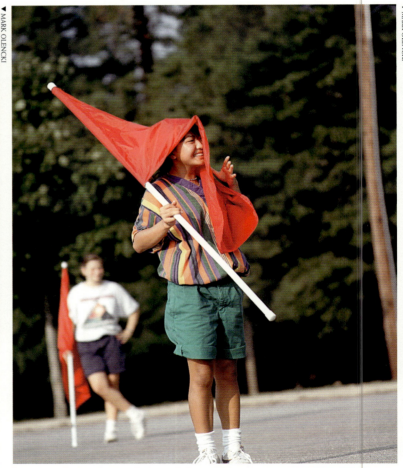

Some of Spartanburg's unique "handi-work"—a high flying pizza at Cosenza's and a renegade flag on the field at Spartanburg High School.

Education in Spartanburg takes a backseat to no one and nothing. The county's 64 public schools serve some 38,000 students, providing programs for the academically gifted as well as assisting those with special learning needs.

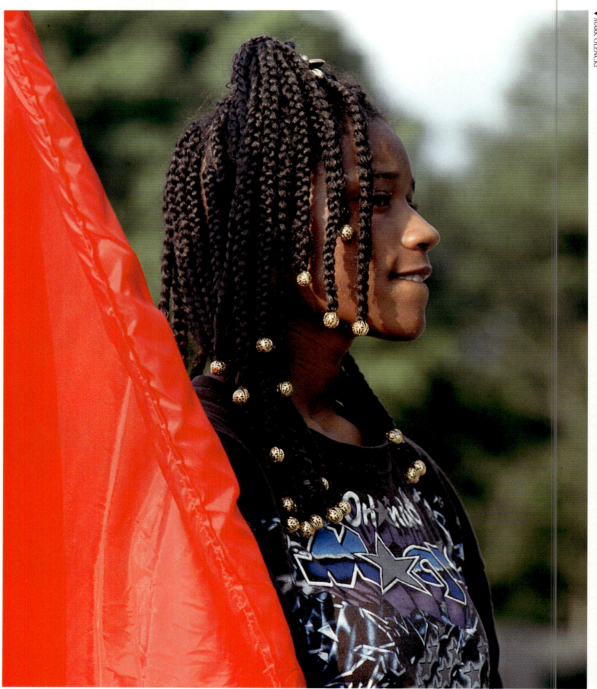

SOUTH CAROLINA PUBLIC SCHO

Portrait of the Good Life

The Arts Center, operated by the Spartanburg Arts Council, offers exposure to the fine arts, dance, and theatre through exhibitions, classes, and presentations year-round. Among the Arts Council staff are Cassandra Baker (opposite left), Executive Director, and Ava Hughes, Director of Special Events.

Wofford College's Olin Building is a state-of-the-art educational facility, housing some of the latest technology used in the classroom, including multimedia, interactive software. However, when students need a break from the computer, they can relax at a more traditional keyboard beneath the portraits in Old Main.

As dusk descends upon Spartanburg, the downtown buildings light up like jewels, giving the city a surge of sparkling vitality.

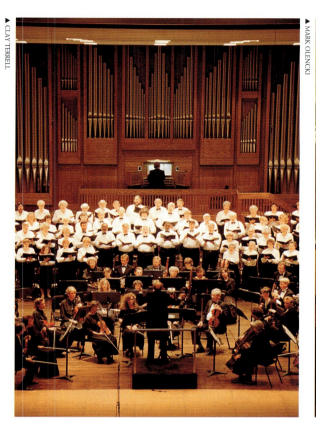

When the sun goes down, the footlights come up. Whether it's entertainment at a corporate gathering or a community fundraiser or a theatre production at Converse College's Twichell Auditorium, you can count on a first-rate performance (opposite).

In addition to a wide range of cultural offerings at Spartanburg Memorial Auditorium—touring Broadway shows, music concerts, and local theatrical productions—there is a repertoire of performances at sites throughout the city, from college theatre at Wofford to the Spartanburg Symphony and Chorus at the Twichell Auditorium (this page).

Springtime in Spartanburg seems to put folks in a celebratory frame of mind, everyone from college graduates to the latest "couple" in town.

No matter what the season or the reason, Spartanburg loves a party. Area festivals and fairs dominate the calendar from spring to fall, including the Fall Arts Festival, Oktoberfest, Skyfest, the Piedmont Interstate Fair, the Poke Sallet Festival in Chesnee, and the Stone Soup Storytelling Festival in Woodruff. But the Spring Fling in downtown Spartanburg remains a perennial favorite, with its arts, crafts, and jazz in the park.

No telling where you'll find Spartanburg on
the move—the March of Dimes Teamwalk,
in-line skating down a country road, or the
bicycle Assault on Mt. Mitchell, a
one-day, 102-mile endurance test that ends
at Mt. Mitchell, the highest point in the
eastern United States.

S P A R T A N B U R G :

If your interest runs toward vintage modes of transportation, you'll find kindred spirits in Spartanburg, especially when Skyfest is in session. The annual aviation event at the Spartanburg Memorial Downtown Airport features barnstorming air shows, hot air balloon races, and helicopter rides, as well as plenty of down-to-earth entertainment.

Some rather interesting characters visit the city from time to time. Most only stay for a day or so, but a few "fashion" individualists, like these folks lounging at the Spring Fling, call Spartanburg home.

SPARTANBURG:

From a fraternity tug-of-war to a Phillies game, Spartanburg has its share of sports heroes and heroes-in-the-making. The Spartanburg Phillies, a Class A South Atlantic League team, has launched more than 100 ballplayers into the major leagues.

To make a decent mud puddle, you need a little water . . . and a few dozen friends to help spread the fun around, like this group of students from Wofford.

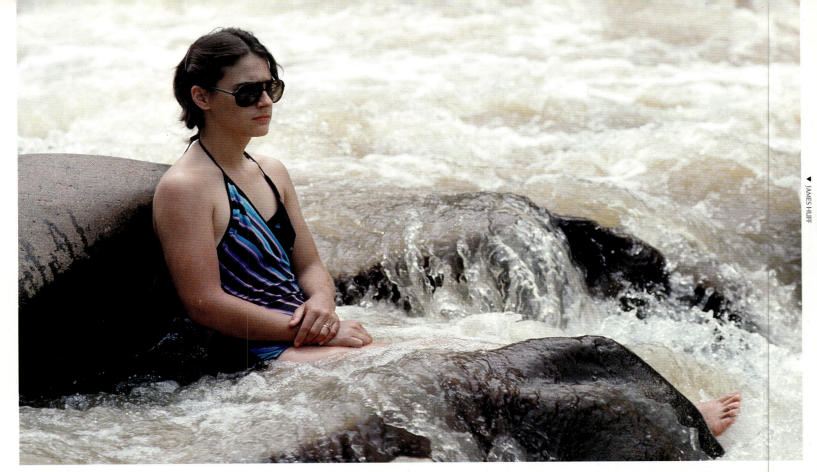

Located in the foothills of the Blue Ridge Mountains, Spartanburg is just a wish away from whitewater rivers and cool mountain lakes. And folks here don't hesitate to take advantage of them.

Sometimes the area's natural beauty strikes
you head on. Other times, you might
have to bend down a bit, get closer to the
earth, to enjoy Mother Nature's
handiwork.

The mountains and foothills of South Carolina are a virtual animal kingdom, but down Highway 29 at Hollywild Animal Park, you'll find some not-so-native species, many of which have retired from film and television. Hollywild is one of the largest private collections of exotic animals in the Southeastern United States, and through its outback safari ride, the park offers "up close and personal" views of a number of wildlife celebrities.

A simple plywood sign and a mountain
backdrop are about all the advertising you
need to attract a crowd of bluegrass lovers.

Agriculture is still an important part of the local economy. Between the rolling hills, you'll find fields blanketed with peach blossoms and, come summer, heavy with fruit. So if you want to see the real Peach State, you need to come to Spartanburg.

pages 92-93

At the end of a clear day, you can see the rest of the world unfold in front of you and feel glad that the view from Spartanburg is so spectacular.

ANDREW PARKER PHOTO

The statue of Revolutionary War General Daniel Morgan was erected in 1881 in Morgan Square, a marketplace and commercial center for area settlers since the late 1700s. Spartanburg was proud to share the bronze likeness, a commemoration of the Battle of Cowpens in 1781, with Philadelphia during the bicentennial celebration of the U.S. Constitution.

SPARTANBURG

Profiles in Excellence

A look at the corporations, businesses, professional groups, and community service organizations that have made this book possible.

BY PEGGY O'NEAL

Hersey Measurement Company

WITH A HISTORY DATING BACK TO THE MID-1800S, HERSEY MEASUREMENT Company is dedicated to innovative solutions to meet the challenges of today's industrial environment. ◆ Hersey Measurement Company products may be found anywhere from the ocean floor to outer space, literally anywhere there is a need for measurement. As technologies become more sophisticated and as the needs for measurement intensify, the Hersey tradition of high-quality

products meets the most exacting requirements.

Hersey's diverse line of measurement instrumentation for water, chemicals, gases, cryogenics (freeze-drying agents), and steam includes flow meters, liquid level tank gauges, Btu systems, electronics, and accessories. As many as several hundred Hersey meters may be found at a single customer location in unlimited line sizes for a variety of uses.

Customer satisfaction is evident from the company's performance. Sales have doubled in the past four years, and Hersey continues to add many products each year. Currently, a new low-cost magnetic flow meter is undergoing field testing and is scheduled for introduction in 1994. This product

will allow the company to enter the existing $110-million magnetic flow market.

AN EXPANDING PRODUCT LINE

From its manufacturing facility at Airport Industrial Park off the bypass on the west side of Spartanburg, Hersey performs design, machining, and testing of its products. As a result of a joint venture with Hydrometer GmbH, a leading manufacturer of meters in Germany, Hersey offers the finest line of turbine meters.

The continually expanding product line now includes a high-temperature meter capable of measuring up to 1,200 degrees Fahrenheit, and Btu systems able to allocate energy usage charges

among individual users within a heating and cooling system, as in apartments or shopping centers. Other special products include a solar-powered flow meter, remote-reading tank-level gauges, and sanitary meters for foods and pharmaceuticals.

Hersey is able to provide this degree of specialized service with the highest possible quality level because of the people making, testing, and shipping the products. The average employee has 16 years of experience with Hersey and takes personal pride in the quality of the company's products and service.

As a privately held company, with its owners intimately involved in every aspect of the business, Hersey is extremely flexible and can respond to specific customer needs immediately. Four of the five owners have measurement backgrounds and understand both the technologies and applications of their products. With complete customer focus and a high level of personal expertise, the employees and owners of Hersey work as a team to develop long-term customer relationships based on product value and trust.

FOUNDED IN 1859

The tradition is more than 130 years in the making. In 1859 Walter Hawes and Charles Hersey formed the firm to manufacture rotary pumps, bolts, and general machinery. Seven years later, Hersey and his brother, Francis, bought out Hawes, and the business continued under the new name of Hersey. The two invented a dryer to be used in the sugar indus-

From its facility at Airport Industrial Park, Hersey performs design, machining, and testing of its products.

As technologies become more sophisticated and as the needs for measurement intensify, Hersey's growing line of high-quality products meets the most exacting requirements.

Originally formed to manufacture rotary pumps, bolts, and general machinery, Hersey boasts a tradition of excellence spanning more than 130 years.

try and began to manufacture sugar, soap, and salt machinery. Water meters were added to the business because of the processes involved. Then other products were added, including steam engines. In fact, Hersey sold the City of Boston its first steam-propelled fire engine in 1875. Today the walls of the company's distinctive Spartanburg headquarters are decorated with pages from Hersey's history, including framed letters of commendation for the products and services provided during both world wars.

Hersey decided in 1972 to focus only on measurement products and acquired Singer American Meter Controls in Spartanburg. Singer's principal products were industrial and residential positive displacement meters.

In 1973 the line was expanded to include liquid level tank gauges to measure tank fluids and temperature levels using mechanical, hydraulic, pneumatic, and electronic methods. The products range from a simple hand pump to a sophisticated system that is able to read up to eight tanks, furnishing tank status, inventory increases, leak test results, product temperature, water level, alarms, and usage information meeting all EPA requirements.

Hersey then purchased Ramapo Instruments Company, which added a line of strain gage flow meters, switches, and process computers, and enabled Hersey to enter new markets. The strain gage meters measure virtually anything—liquids, gases, even steam. From half-inch to unlimited line sizes, from -320 degrees to +500 degrees Fahrenheit and pressure up to 10,000 psi, the strain gage flow meter is flexible and adaptable to meet a variety of industrial and commercial uses.

In 1987 Hersey was acquired by an Atlanta, Georgia, corporation and is now a division of Flow Measurement, Inc. The owners decided to keep Hersey in Spartanburg because of the excellent work force. The company also built a new plant on Venture Boulevard and acquired enough property to double the size of its facilities.

Through 174 domestic and 40 international distributors, products of Hersey Measurement Company are at work for most Fortune 500 firms and numerous industries. And Hersey is poised to continue its innovation and customer-focused service for the century to come. "We are knowledgeable, experienced, and absolutely dedicated to service," says Pat Mullen, president and one of the owners. "Our entire future is based on working hand in hand with our customers to develop the products they need, with assurance of delivery, quality, and dependability."

Milliken & Company

SPARTANBURG-BASED MILLIKEN & COMPANY IS ONE OF THE WORLD'S LARGEST TEXTILE companies and a leader in research, technology, quality, and customer service. Milliken's 14,000 associates work from 55 manufacturing locations worldwide to create more than 48,000 textile and chemical products. ◆ Milliken products can be found in almost every aspect of life. Milliken carpets provide comfort, style, and long wear in hotels, businesses, and public areas throughout the world. Its fabrics keep soldiers

and youngsters warm, astronauts safe, and major league baseball players comfortable; other fabrics are found in cars, sailboats, tennis balls, and printer ribbons. Chemicals developed by Milliken give Crayola crayons and markers their color and automobile dashboards their durability. Other Milliken chemicals are used in see-through

NEW ENGLAND ROOTS
In 1865 in Portland, Maine, Seth Milliken and William Deering founded a woolen fabrics jobbing firm, the Deering Milliken Company. William Deering left the company a few years later and started the Deering Harvester Company, which is today known as Navistar.

year on Milliken's Southern manufacturing operations grew.

In 1954 the company moved its headquarters from New York to a new facility in Spartanburg. The sprawling and handsomely landscaped grounds along I-85 and I-585 today feature ponds and public areas for picnicking, walking or jogging, bird-watching, and other

Colorful fabrics are displayed in the Roger Milliken Research and Customer Center (above).

The entire community enjoys the fountains, ponds, and grounds of Milliken & Company's research and corporate headquarters (right).

aspirin bottles and food storage containers.

Working directly with customers such as Hyatt Regency, Opryland, L.L. Bean, Ford Motor Company, McDonald's, and crayon manufacturer Binney & Smith, company researchers strive for new solutions and develop new products at Milliken Research Center in Spartanburg, the largest private research organization in the world.

In 1868 Seth Milliken moved the company headquarters to New York City, at that time the heart of the American textile industry. Deering Milliken prospered in New York, and from its northern base decided to invest in the emerging Southern textile industry. In 1884 he invested in a plant that was built by the Montgomery family at Pacolet, in the southern part of Spartanburg County, and from that

recreational activities. The Milliken headquarters has set the standard for many other area corporations and the Greenville-Spartanburg Airport, which have added their own attractive landscaping.

In 1976 Deering Milliken changed its name to Milliken & Company. Today, after 125 years of leadership in state-of-the-art manufacturing processes and equipment, Milliken & Company has

manufacturing and sales locations in the United States, Canada, Belgium, France, Denmark, England, and Japan, as well as licensing agreements in Australia.

Milliken is known worldwide for its ongoing Pursuit of Excellence process, instituted in 1981. Chairman of the Board Roger Milliken devotes more than half of his time to the effort, which has resulted in industry acclaim and hundreds of major customer quality awards. Among these are the Malcolm Baldrige National Quality Award, the British Quality Award, the Canada Awards for Business Excellence, and in 1993, the European Quality Award in its second year of existence. Milliken was the first fabric supplier to receive General Motors' Spear 1 Award, the first Ford Motor Co. supplier to be honored with that company's Q-1 Award, and the only fabric supplier to receive the Chrysler Pentastar Award.

ENVIRONMENTAL EXCELLENCE

As one of only 25 charter members of the Encouraging Environmental Excellence Program of the American Textile Manufacturers Institute, Milliken follows a 10-point plan of environmental achievements. These include commitments to en-

vironmental policies, supplier and customer outreach, environmental audits, close cooperation with government, and associate and community involvement.

Invited in 1990 to participate in a federal program calling for a 50 percent reduction of certain chemical wastes by the year 1995, Milliken has already reduced many of these to zero. The company was the first textile firm in America to eliminate chlorinated solvents by using organic alternatives, and has successfully converted water sludge to bio-fuel. Its aggressive program to reduce water consumption has been highly successful, and since 1989 the company has reduced the solid waste sent to landfills by 65 percent.

Milliken's goal is to be a good corporate citizen, which means more than simply complying with environmental laws. Its commitment extends to every process of every function of the company, including providing centralized collection of home recyclables for associates. Milliken is committed to striving for zero waste generation to land, air, and water.

COMMITTED TO EDUCATION

Milliken & Company considers itself a partner with the educational

services of the communities in which it operates. Every plant location is partnering in programs with local school districts in efforts to cultivate the full potential of the young people in its communities.

Associates themselves are encouraged to seek out education and training. And opportunities abound—hundreds of short courses and intensive studies are offered through Milliken University at the company's headquarters in Spartanburg. The rationale behind this emphasis is that associates who grow in understanding can bring new talents to their work, family lives, and communities, thus creating an environment for excellence in every aspect of their lives.

The progressive, innovative idea that continuing education can help nurture excellence is a cornerstone of Milliken's business philosophy. Though the company has many ways of recognizing innovation among associates, the ultimate kudos is induction into the Innovators Hall of Fame, established in 1984. This award honors associates for new ideas, methods, or devices that cause advances in knowledge or improvements in techniques and have significant relative worth, utility, or importance to Milliken.

The Milliken Arboretum (top left) includes several walking/exercise trails. Physical fitness is encouraged through the Milliken Health & Fitness Center.

Customers enjoy the serene beauty and hospitality of the Milliken Guest House (top right).

Milliken University (above) is just one example of the company's commitment to education and lifelong learning.

Carolina Club Properties

A Division of Milliken & Company

COMMITTED TO THE CONTINUED DEVELOPMENT OF THE FINEST RESIDENTIAL COMMUNITY in the Upstate, Carolina Club Properties, a division of Milliken & Company, offers homes and homesites in the Carolina Country Club Community. ◆ In 1988 Carolina Club Properties initiated its development activities by a careful study of how best to utilize some of the most pristine woodlands in South Carolina. Several of the country's best developers were consulted and many subdivisions were visited,

Nature in harmony with an elegant, relaxed lifestyle: The rolling hills of Carolina Country Club Community provide a convenient haven in one of the Southeast's fastest growing business areas. Homes are located along the 18-hole championship golf course, on a quiet lake, or on a peaceful cul-de-sac.

resulting in a handsome residential area surrounding one of South Carolina's finest country clubs. It encompasses 1,600 acres and is dedicated to the preservation of a peaceful and informal, yet elegant lifestyle.

Carolina Country Club Community's attractive homes are located along the 18-hole championship golf course, on a quiet lake, or on a peaceful cul-de-sac. Several streams wander through the land; deer and wild turkey roam the wooded areas. The different development phases offer houses of various sizes and price levels. An architectural review committee approves the house siting, plans, and landscaping—ensuring a harmonious blend of architectural styles.

With a deep appreciation of nature, Carolina Country Club Community is served by underground utilities, public water, and public sewer. Entrance is through a security gate, which is staffed 24 hours a day. Broad roads with storm drainage, curbs, and street lighting are flanked by spacious

green areas that complement the residential landscaping.

Diversity marks Carolina Country Club Community; intermixed with Southern drawls are the accents of many cultures. Empty nesters, retirees, and young families enjoy the walking and jogging trails, bike rides, visiting friends, or gathering at the Family Center. The Family Center features a multipurpose athletic field and a covered pavilion, with large grills for outdoor cooking and oyster roasts. Individual grills and picnic tables are nestled along a clear flowing stream. Soccer, baseball or softball, badminton, volleyball, horseshoes, and basketball can all be enjoyed on the sports field.

Available to all its members is the Carolina Country Club, one of the South's premier full-service clubs. The 6,784-yard championship golf course is ranked among the best in the state, with active ladies and juniors golf groups. Ten tennis courts are available to members day and night. Younger family members participate in the swim

team, which holds practice in the club's pool and competes with neighboring clubs during the summer.

Holly Hall, a country club facility available to all property owners, is an 8,000-square-foot, beam-and-peg structure designed for dances, receptions, meetings, and special events. Dining facilities offer superb choices served in a casual grill, formal dining room, or rooms able to accommodate small or large groups.

The rolling hills of Carolina Country Club Community provide a convenient haven in one of the Southeast's fastest growing business areas. Located just seven miles from downtown Spartanburg, this residential area is only 25 miles from the Greenville-Spartanburg Airport and offers easy access to the cultural, educational, and athletic opportunities of the area.

Nature in harmony with an elegant, relaxed lifestyle makes Carolina Country Club Community a unique living community.

Butler, Means, Evins & Browne

FOR OVER A CENTURY, THE LAW FIRM OF BUTLER, MEANS, EVINS & BROWNE AND ITS PREDE-cessor firms have been engaged in the general practice of law in Spartanburg and the surrounding area. Throughout its prestigious history, the firm has produced a justice of the U.S. Supreme Court, three judges of the U.S. Court of Appeals for the Fourth Circuit, and a United States District Judge in South Carolina. In addition, two of its attorneys have served as United States Senators, two as Governor of South Carolina, and one as a United States Congressman.

PRACTICE AREAS

For the past 40 years, the firm has been principally concerned with a general civil practice representing large utilities, numerous corporations, insurance companies, banks, and individuals. The firm also represents two public entities: the Commissioners of Public Works of the City of Spartanburg and the Greenville-Spartanburg Airport Commission.

Butler, Means, Evins & Browne also has a varied and active trial practice in all courts and appears regularly before city and county councils, the South Carolina Industrial Commission (where it represents the largest workers' compensation insurance carrier in Spartanburg County), and many other agencies.

Several of the firm's 10 attorneys and counselors participate in domestic relations, estate planning and trusts, probate, construction, product liability, medical malpractice, debtor/creditor, and criminal law, and skilled preparation of the necessary documentation to support a large real estate practice.

"We have a rich heritage and a strong background in the Spartanburg area. Our firm has been representing all types of corporate, public, and individual interests in this community for over 100 years," says partner Robert E. Browne III. "The current practice has certainly inherited clients over the years, but we are continually striving to build new client relationships. One large client has been with us for more than 70 years, and another client, a leading bank, has used the firm continuously since it reopened after the Great Depression. On the other hand, we have new clients walking through our doors almost every day."

The firm has secured these relationships through a seemingly simple philosophy. "We work hard, and we do our homework," Browne says. "Whether it's a case or a contract or simply giving advice, we are willing to do whatever it takes to get the information the client needs."

Much of that information comes from the law library at the firm's offices on North Church Street near the courthouse in downtown Spartanburg. The legal library is the largest in the commu-nity, and the principals often provide attorneys from other practices access to its extensive collection.

Through the years, as principals in the firm have retired or moved on to other activities, Butler, Means, Evins & Browne has

been selective in choosing quality replacements. "We've recruited good scholars with outstanding academic and work records that are in keeping with the needs of our clientele," Browne states.

And although the trend in law is to specialize, Butler, Means, Evins & Browne intends to remain a general practice. "We associate specialists when the need arises," Browne adds, "but we believe a solid general practice is the basis of our continued success."

The firm's attorneys and counselors conduct a general civil practice representing large utilities, numerous corporations, insurance companies, banks, and individuals.

Spartan Mills

S PARTANBURG COUNTY'S ECONOMY HAS GROWN AND DIVERSIFIED OVER THE PAST CEN-
tury, but two facts have remained constant: the textile industry is still the area's
largest employer, and Spartan Mills provides more jobs in the county than any
other textile company. Spartan Mills employs 4,500 people in the Carolinas,
Georgia, and New York, but nearly half of those individuals work in the company's seven
Spartanburg County operations. ◆ Another constant is the Montgomery family, which

has controlled and managed Spartan Mills since its founding. Captain John H. Montgomery established the company in Spartanburg in 1890. Today his grandson, Walter Montgomery Sr., is chairman of the board, and his great-grandson, Walter Montgomery Jr., is president.

RESPONDING TO INDUSTRY CHANGE

Amid a continuing surge of imported fabrics that began three decades ago, Spartan Mills is on the leading edge of technological changes critical to the strength of the U.S. textile industry. "We are dedicated to providing jobs in this industry that is so vital to our national economy," says Walter Montgomery Jr.

For years Spartan Mills produced primarily greige (unfinished) goods and corduroys, but in the past 30 years it began a diversification process through investments in new technology, equipment, and employee training. As a result, the company today primarily produces finished and printed fabrics used for clothing and home furnishings.

At its plants, Spartan Mills manufactures the creations of many of today's best-known home designers whose fabrics are sold domestically and, increasingly, to upscale markets throughout the world. The company also provides fabrics for a number of domestic labels in high-end knit and woven leisure apparel, as well as for the British retailing powerhouse, Marks & Spencer. One division, which is devoted to the health care industry, manufactures fabrics for hospital blankets, drapes, surgical wear, and uniforms, among other items. Spartan Mills recently signed a long-term partnership agreement with the world's leading supplier of health care products.

The company also produces for the highly competitive markets of nonwoven fabrics, where end uses are as varied as landfill liners, furniture interiors, and carpet backings.

Says President Montgomery, "We are a company responding to market changes. This begins with our people, who have risen to the challenge of education and training. It is supported by our constant attention to technological change, and it is founded in our determination to be a leader in world markets for decades to come."

AN INDUSTRY AND COMMUNITY LEADER

The company's contribution to the industry as well as to the Spartanburg community is long-standing, varied, and colorful. Spartan Mills was one of the founding companies of the American Textile Manufacturers Institute, the world's largest textile association, and the Institute of Textile Technology, the industry's primary research arm.

Chairman of the Board Walter Montgomery Sr. is often referred to as "Mr. Spartanburg" because of the many leadership roles he has assumed during his career of more than 70 years. His commitment to furthering new opportunities in the arts, education, and business, as well as to programs that meet basic human needs, has also been an important thrust for the company. During its long history as a leading business in Spartanburg, Spartan Mills has supported community efforts through generous funding and employee volunteers.

OLENCKI GRAPHICS

Captain John H. Montgomery established Spartan Mills in 1890. Today his grandson, Walter Montgomery Sr. (right), is chairman of the board, and his great-grandson, Walter Montgomery Jr., is president.

Southern Bell

A S SPARTANBURG HAS GROWN AS AN INTERNATIONAL COMMUNITY, BOASTING MORE PER capita foreign investment than any other community in the nation, some very important changes have taken place. One significant behind-the-scenes development has been the enhanced services provided by Southern Bell. ◆ "The services we provide in the Spartanburg area can compete with the finest of telecommunications services anywhere in the world," says J.H. "Jim" Thomas Jr., manager of corporate and

external affairs for the five-county region served from the company's Spartanburg offices.

Offering the latest in telecommunications technology, Southern Bell in the Spartanburg area also is prepared for the next century with 100 percent digital switching and a 400-mile fiber-optic network in place. On the horizon for the near future are services such as video transmissions and simultaneous voice and data communications.

Southern Bell has three locations in Spartanburg, including the main office downtown at Broadwalk, another downtown office at East Main and Pine, and a work center on Belton Drive in west Spartanburg. Based at these various locations are the engineering department, primarily responsible for designing circuits; a network organization for switching calls; a construction group to install and construct lines; technicians to connect and maintain the lines; and long-distance operators for handling some intrastate calls.

COMMUNITY LEADERSHIP

"The future of our company from both employee and customer standpoints lies in what we can do to enhance our schools, improve the business climate, and support the quality of life in this area," says Thomas.

Southern Bell's commitment is visible throughout the community. For example, the Telephone Pioneers of America, a national non-profit organization composed of employees of Bell companies, is the largest employee service organization in the world. The local chapter sponsors a room at the Children's

Embracing the technology of the future, employees take part in a video conference with a colleague from across the state.

Southern Bell employees engineer new lines for customers using a computer-aided design system (below left).

Locally, the Telephone Pioneers of America participate in "Beep Ball" games for visually handicapped youth.

Shelter, a temporary home for abused or displaced children where once a month the volunteers throw a party for the children. The Pioneers also provide "Hug-a-Bears" for young victims of trauma via the fire and police departments, hospitals, and rescue squads; sponsor "Beep Ball," a special game for visually impaired students, at the South Carolina School for the Deaf and the Blind; and sponsor the regional Rainbow Games for physically handicapped students.

In the area of education, Southern Bell sponsors the Teacher Mini-Grant Program, which funds special projects for elementary and high school teachers. The company also helped start Spartanburg's Cities in Schools, an alternative school for junior high students at

risk of becoming high school dropouts. And Southern Bell helps improve the lives and ambitions of the area's young people through Junior Achievement, Boy Scouts of America, Career Days, and the Business-Education Partnerships program that encourages businesses to share their human and other resources with local schools.

Southern Bell also provides both volunteer and monetary support for the United Way of the Piedmont and for the visual and performing arts through the Arts Council of Spartanburg County.

"We have a communications network that's second to none in South Carolina," Thomas says, "and we're proud to serve in many other ways a community that's second to none."

Inman Mills

INMAN MILLS HAS BEEN AN ESTABLISHED LEADER IN THE TEXTILE INDUSTRY FOR MORE THAN 90 years, producing high-quality greige (unfinished) goods for home furnishings, apparel, and other end uses. Although a shopper examining upholstered furniture or new clothes will not find the Inman Mills name on any products, the company's quiet strength permeates the textile industry. ◆ Founded in 1902 by James A. Chapman, Inman Mills has maintained its original base in the Spartanburg area. The company today

The company uses modern equipment to produce high-quality greige (unfinished) goods for home furnishings, apparel, and other end uses.

Founded in 1902 by James A. Chapman (right), Inman Mills is today owned and operated by the third and fourth generations of the Chapman family.

OLENCKI GRAPHICS

employs more than 1,000 people at its Inman and Saybrook plants in Inman (20 miles north of Spartanburg) and at its Riverdale, Mountain Shoals, and Ramey plants in Enoree in southern Spartanburg County. The company is owned and operated by the third and fourth generations of the Chapman family, who continue a longtime tradition of caring about employees, offering flexibility and versatility to the customer, and producing the highest quality product at competitive prices.

But Inman Mills is equally committed to the future. To that end, the company is actively involved in developing tomorrow's products and processes through membership in numerous national and industry groups.

SUPPORTING EMPLOYEES AND THE COMMUNITY

The dedicated employees of Inman Mills share the company's pride in its competitive edge. With their innovative thinking, willingness to move forward with new concepts, and never-ending thirst for problem-solving, they are the

driving force behind the company's success.

Since the beginning, Inman Mills has returned that dedication by actively supporting the communities in which it operates. The company's two recreation centers offer employees and their families access to bowling alleys, meeting rooms, kitchens, and game rooms. Likewise, Inman Mills maintains its own outdoor recreational facilities outfitted with tennis courts, playgrounds, sports fields, basketball courts, and shady picnic areas.

Inman Mills was the first industrial firm in South Carolina to provide free immunizations to infants through on-site clinics in cooperation with the state's immunization program. This service has brought improved prospects for good health to thousands of families in the northern and southern portions of Spartanburg County.

Since 1946 Inman Riverdale Foundation, a nonprofit organization formed to support education,

has endowed schools and churches and has awarded undergraduate and nursing scholarships. The company also offers generous support to local Little League and scouting programs, and is a long-standing benefactor of the United Way, Junior Achievement, March of Dimes, Music Foundation, Mobile Meals, American Heart Association, and American Cancer Society, among others.

From community service to modern manufacturing processes, quality is an important part of everything done at Inman Mills. The company works to offer a better quality of life in Spartanburg County through education, awareness, and support, and it strives to produce the highest quality products by investing in the latest textile technologies and advanced training for employees. It is this commitment to quality in action that will pave the way to the future at Inman Mills.

Spartanburg Coca-Cola Bottling Company

ALTHOUGH MOST HOMES IN SPARTANBURG HAVE A TWO-LITER BOTTLE OF COCA-COLA in the refrigerator, few residents know that it was a local enterprise, Spartanburg Coca-Cola Bottling Company, that helped launch the recyclable plastic bottle. ◆ R.G. Johnston Jr., president of Spartanburg Coca-Cola Bottling Company, remembers well the challenge of introducing the world to the two-liter bottle in 1977. "We had determined that the market wanted a larger 'package' to use at home,"

Johnston recalls. For over a year, the Spartanburg team worked hand-in-hand with plastic manufacturers and the Coca-Cola Company of Atlanta, Georgia, producer of the world-renowned soft drink syrup.

"When the pilot project was complete and the product finally came to market, it was problem-free and very well accepted," Johnston says.

REFRESHING THE COMMUNITY FOR NINE DECADES

With 152 employees today, Spartanburg Coca-Cola has been a leader in the community since opening its first plant in 1903. The company's current downtown facilities at 500 West Main Street were constructed in 1936.

As a primary sponsor of the annual Spring Fling Arts and Music Festival, Spartanburg Coca-Cola maintains a very visible presence. Behind the scenes, the company also supports nearly every aspect of the community, including Meals on Wheels, the Spartanburg County Fair, the Charles Lea Center for the mentally and emotionally handicapped, the Spartanburg Phillies Class A baseball farm team, and dozens of other efforts to improve the local quality of life.

While many businesses have moved to locations outside the city, Spartanburg Coca-Cola has continued to be a fixture in the downtown area. "We have a close working relationship with the city, and we enjoy being part of the fabric of downtown," says Johnston. "It's very important to us to maintain relationships that tell the community we care."

SERVICE THAT LEADS THE MARKET

Spartanburg Coca-Cola is a franchised bottler of Coca-Cola Bottling Company United, Inc., the fifth largest Coca-Cola bottler in the country. With headquarters in Birmingham, Alabama, and plants in cities throughout the Southeast, the company purchases the famous syrup from the Coca-Cola Company.

"Very few local franchises actually 'bottle' anymore," explains Johnston. "We depend on our sister plants to can and bottle the product. In Spartanburg, we are primarily a distributor and service provider."

And over the years, the company has become known for its excellent service. In fact, Spartanburg Coca-Cola is currently the market leader in a franchise area of approximately 230,000 people. Its array of Coca-Cola products includes Dr. Pepper, Sprite, A&W Root Beer, Nu-Grape, SunKist, PowerAde sports drinks, Nestea, and Minute Maid juices. Johnston points with pride to the fact that most of the products are packaged in recyclable containers—another indication of how seriously the company takes its corporate responsibility.

Since 1957 Spartanburg Coca-Cola has also operated Automatic Buffets Incorporated (ABI), a subsidiary that serves industrial and commercial machine vending operations and cafeterias.

"Coca-Cola has a mystique about it. Everyone's interested in it, and that makes it a fun business,"

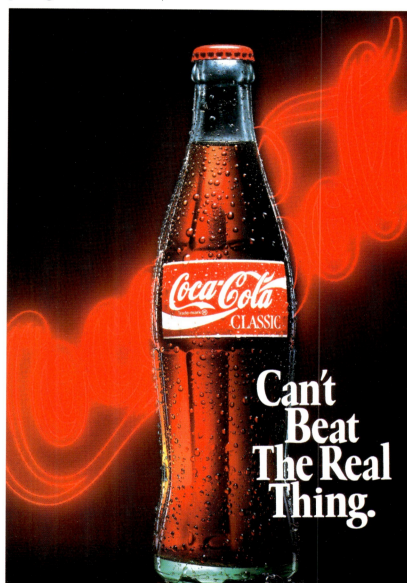

Johnston says. "Our employees appreciate that fact and work together in a family-like atmosphere to achieve the excellence expected of the world's most widely recognized trademark."

With 152 employees today, Spartanburg Coca-Cola has been a leader in the community since opening its first plant in 1903.

105

Duke Power

RELIABLE ENERGY IS VITAL TO SPARTANBURG AND UPSTATE SOUTH CAROLINA, A GROWing area with one of the highest percentages of manufacturing employment in the nation. As the country's seventh largest investor-owned electric utility, Duke Power embraces the challenge of serving the needs of commercial, industrial, and residential consumers throughout the region. ◆ "Duke Power is answering the push for change in our industry and in the Carolinas by becoming a more customer-driven,

cost-effective, and responsive company," says William S. Lee, chairman and president.

To that end, the company is actively working with large customers to develop effective and efficient energy management plans, as well as with individual consumers to meet today's competitive challenges and energy needs. In addition, Duke Power has put in place safeguards for the protection of the environment and wildlife,

The employees of Duke Power are committed to good citizenship and community service, especially in the area of educational programs.

Commercial and industrial customers, such as Milliken & Company (right), are assisted by Duke Power's team of energy specialists.

and conducts workshops to help classroom teachers provide relevant and stimulating science materials for students.

MEETING THE REGION'S ENERGY NEEDS

Duke Power, which began doing business in 1905, established its Spartanburg office in 1929. Headquartered in Charlotte, North Carolina, the company today serves approximately 1.7 million residential, general service, and industrial customers. The Spartanburg regional office on West Main Street employs 230

people and serves 120,000 residential and industrial customers in Spartanburg and neighboring counties.

Duke Power operates eight coal-fired stations, 27 hydroelectric stations, and three nuclear stations. For 17 of the past 18 years, the company has operated the most efficient coal-fired system in the country. It also is the only investor-owned utility to design and build its own power plants, resulting in construction costs that are well below the national average. "Industrial customers of Duke Power find that they are more competitive and cost-effective because our energy costs are low," says Lee.

In its quest for excellence, Duke Power strives to provide individualized services and innovative programs for its customers. Commercial and industrial customers may take advantage of a team of energy specialists who will analyze procedures and recommend efficiencies for energy management. Innovative energy management programs for residential consumers, such as time-of-use rates and interruptible service rate programs, also translate into savings both on current power bills and in the long term by delaying construction of expensive new generators.

A GOOD CORPORATE CITIZEN

"Duke Power has a strong commitment to good citizenship and community service, especially in the area of educational programs," says David E. White, district manager for Spartanburg. For example, the company was instrumental in setting up homework centers for

elementary students in all seven school districts in Spartanburg County and in three Cherokee County schools, a project recognized by the South Carolina Department of Education in 1992-93. The Spartanburg office also offers and conducts the "Developmental Partners" program for college-bound minority students, a monthly night course focusing on important nonacademic subjects such as budgeting and successful job interview skills.

"Duke Power has a rich history in Spartanburg and this region of the Carolinas," White says. "We will continue to build on that legacy through our focus on innovative energy programs and community commitment."

Grier & Company, Inc.

JAMES C. GRIER FOUNDED GRIER & COMPANY IN 1913 TO PROVIDE INSURANCE SERVICES FOR the citizens of Spartanburg, then a small town with a growing textile industry. As Spartanburg has expanded and diversified, so too has this homegrown company, which the Grier family has helped manage since its founding. Today Grier & Company, Inc. is the largest independently owned insurance agency in Spartanburg and operates one of the oldest and most respected real estate agencies in the city.

BUILDING THE FAMILY BUSINESS

Soon after World War I, James Grier was joined in his efforts to build the insurance business by his brother, L.A. Grier. Following World War II, when L.A. Grier's sons, Tom and L.A. Jr., joined the company, the family realized it could meet other needs in the community and seize an opportunity. Consequently, Grier & Company formed a real estate division to help provide the new homes and property that were in demand as servicemen returned to the area and new businesses started up and began to flourish.

Ranny Brown was named broker-in-charge of the Real Estate Division in 1946 and has been its president since 1972 when Grier & Company was incorporated. For almost 50 years, the firm has been a leading real estate agency in the community, handling residential property. Adding to the company's strength has been its affiliation with PHH HOMEQUITY, Inc., the largest third-party corporate home buyer in the nation.

The history of the insurance business side of the company also has been one of growth, particularly in the past 30 years. Grier & Company began expanding its product line in the 1950s and '60s as businesses and corporations from Europe and Asia began to establish marketing headquarters and manufacturing operations in Spartanburg County. "The company's long history and tradition of quality made it a natural choice for the many individuals and companies moving to the area that were seeking insur-

ance services," says Tom Grier, chairman of the board.

As a result of its rapid growth, Grier & Company today is listed among the top 3 percent of all independent insurance agencies in the nation. To further expand its market presence, the firm opened offices in Greenville and Union, South Carolina. In addition, the company has associated with numerous organizations throughout the world that provide access to a

variety of insurance services and products. Harry C. Morris Jr. is president of the Insurance Division, which employs 30 people.

"Although the dimensions of the organization have grown from hometown to international, the focus of Grier & Company has not changed," Grier says. The company remains committed to giving the client—large or small, personal, commercial, or industrial—the most efficient customer service, the

best insurance coverage and claims assistance, and the highest quality real estate services.

Adds Grier, "We continue to challenge ourselves with building our knowledge and resources in order to provide the best services possible."

With this in mind, Grier & Company has combined its Insurance Division with Riedman Corporation of Rochester, New York, and is now among the 20 largest

independently owned agencies in the United States. With over 53 locations, the companies are able to utilize the strength of their combined size and expand both the variety of services and number of markets from which to choose.

Grier & Company and Riedman Corporation together will continue a tradition of service to meet the changing insurance needs of the Upstate.

The firm's leadership includes (from left) W. Randolph Brown, president, Real Estate Division; Harry C. Morris Jr., president, Insurance Division; and J. Tom Grier, chairman of the board and president of the corporation.

Spartanburg Area Chamber of Commerce

I**T WAS 107 DAYS TO REMEMBER. BETWEEN MARCH AND JUNE OF 1992, THE SPARTANBURG AREA** Chamber of Commerce worked hand in hand with state and local leaders to pluck the biggest economic plum ever for South Carolina—BMW's first U.S. manufacturing facility. ◆ As the clock ticked on the state's bid for the German automaker, the chamber, along with local developers and state and county officials, put together a package with exactly what BMW wanted—1,000 acres of land, interstate highway exposure, and easy

access to a major airport. Three months of almost nonstop work paid off when South Carolina Governor Carroll Campbell received a much-welcomed fax from Munich declaring Spartanburg as the site for BMW Manufacturing Corp.

The announcement marked another milestone in the chamber's history of successful economic development efforts. In fact, Spartanburg was ranked first in the state in terms of job creation for

BOLSTERING THE LOCAL ECONOMY

Diversification is at the heart of the chamber's efforts today. Once primarily dependent on agriculture and textiles, Spartanburg had the foresight in the 1960s to undertake vigorous corporate recruitment. Since then, the area has lured the largest per capita diversified international base in the United States. Spartanburg County is home to the headquarters, distribution centers,

company the largest service-sector employer in South Carolina. Achieving the chamber's mission requires more than recruiting employers. It involves hundreds of volunteers and touches education, quality improvement, community and leadership development, beautification, and small-business development.

The chamber is a catalyst for business involvement in education at all levels, with the goal of maxi-

The chamber's headquarters at the corner of North Pine and St. John streets is also home to the Spartanburg Convention and Visitors Bureau.

Leadership Spartanburg recently traveled to historic Walnut Grove (above right).

seven of the eight years between 1984 and 1992. When BMW announced its $400-million investment, which would create about 2,000 new jobs, the chamber began preparing for the spinoff effects. It has been estimated that BMW's presence will have an economic impact of more than $1 billion and will create more than 10,000 jobs over the next two decades.

or manufacturing facilities of more than 80 international firms representing more than 13 countries.

The local economy also has benefited from new employers in ceramics, printing, foods, packaging, automotive components, electronics, and a host of other industries. In the late 1980s the chamber assisted TW Services, now Flagstar Companies, Inc., as it consolidated Chicago and West Coast operations in Spartanburg, making the

mizing work force potential and enhancing the area's quality of life. Recent efforts include Spartanburg 2000 in which representatives of business and education are moving the community toward national goals for educational improvement. Similarly, Cities in Schools is a dropout prevention program involving a partnership of the education, business, and human services sectors in Spartanburg. Another chamber program, Top Priority:

Education, encourages local businesses to commit to practices that support education.

The chamber also monitors governmental affairs and public policy, always staying abreast of how proposed changes or enactments of local, state, and federal laws might affect the business community. The chamber's Public Policy Committee is a proactive force in helping to study and propose legislation on issues important to business.

To benefit existing employers, the chamber in 1984 began a Quality in the Workplace program, which has been recognized as one of the top programs of its kind in the country. Focusing at first only on manufacturers, the program now reaches out to service businesses and nonprofit organizations that are seeking continuous quality improvement.

SERVING A GROWING MEMBERSHIP

The chamber's 1,800 members can take advantage of a range of activities, programs, and services. Enhancing these efforts are the seven Area Councils of the chamber, which provide forums for the diverse regional interests of the 830-square-mile county and its 13 municipalities.

The chamber offers leadership seminars to provide supervisors, managers, and executives with hands-on training in human relations and labor law. A Minority Business/Professional Committee promotes programs and opportunities for minority small-business development, while the annual Small Business Exposition encourages businesses to exhibit their products and services to potential customers. Leadership Spartanburg is an aggressive community awareness and leadership training effort designed to help identify potential leaders and enlighten them to the services and needs of all segments of the community.

The chamber also coordinates seminars, workshops, and networking opportunities for its members. These include a monthly Business After Hours social mixer hosted by member organizations; periodic breakfast meetings in which specific issues are explored; and seminars on topics such as international taxation and workers' compensation.

Services and publications available to the chamber's membership include economic and demographic information, grand opening assistance, legislative bill status reports, newcomer assistance, and the Service Corps of Retired Executives, which provides free counseling to small businesses in the area.

The chamber's headquarters at the corner of North Pine and St. John streets is also home to the Spartanburg Convention and Visitors Bureau, which provides assistance to individuals and to groups hosting athletic, cultural, or business events in the county. Also housed there is Spartanburg Community Events, a nonprofit umbrella organization that produces the local Spring Fling and International festivals.

Although the beginnings of the Spartanburg Area Chamber of Commerce date back to the turn of the century, the organization was officially chartered in 1918, an event commemorated by a Diamond Anniversary celebration in 1993. As it moves forward to greet the next century, the chamber renews its commitment to economic development, nurtured by cooperation and dedication to the vitality of Spartanburg County.

Above left: Chamber leadership for the future includes John Poole (left), 1995 chairman of the board, and Dr. Paul Foerster, 1994 chairman.

Above right: Ben Haskew (left), chamber president, and Dr. Sidney Fulmer, 1993 chairman.

109

The Hospitals of Spartanburg County

THE FOUR HOSPITALS OF SPARTANBURG COUNTY ARE TECHNOLOGICAL LEADERS WITH A caring touch. Working cooperatively to provide a comprehensive array of services, they are dedicated to promoting good health as well as treating illness and injury with professionalism and personal compassion. All are fully accredited by the Joint Commission for the Accreditation of Healthcare Organizations (JCAHO). ◆ Hospital services in the county are provided by B.J. Workman Memorial

Hospital in Woodruff and Doctors Memorial Hospital, Mary Black Memorial Hospital, and Spartanburg Regional Medical Center in Spartanburg.

at Workman Hospital performed Upstate South Carolina's first "belly button" gall bladder surgery in May 1990, using fiber-optic technology. In addition to other surgical

Doctors Memorial was the first hospital in the Southeast to provide second-generation kidney stone lithotripsy. The hospital also boasts the Ophthalmic Laser Center, the

The four hospitals of Spartanburg County are (from left) B.J. Workman Memorial Hospital, Doctors Memorial Hospital, Mary Black Memorial Hospital, and Spartanburg Regional Medical Center.

B.J. WORKMAN MEMORIAL HOSPITAL

Serving almost 11,000 patients annually, B.J. Workman Memorial Hospital is a 43-bed, acute-care community hospital located in Woodruff to serve southern Spartanburg County and surrounding counties.

Workman Hospital opened its doors in 1955, funded in large part by donations of a day's pay from the employees of area textile mills. In 1967 it expanded from 34 to 43 beds. The hospital's most recent addition, completed in 1991, provides private rooms and enhanced service areas.

Services of the hospital include an emergency department, respiratory and physical therapy, surgery, radiology, endoscopy, and an extensive laboratory. Surgeons

procedures, the hospital performs endoscopies to check for ulcers and colon cancer.

DOCTORS MEMORIAL HOSPITAL

Doctors Memorial Hospital, with 108 beds including private accommodations, was opened in 1966 as a skilled nursing facility for long-term care. In 1973 Doctors Memorial began functioning as an independent, privately owned hospital after extensive remodeling and the addition of a three-story wing for surgery and ancillary services. Located on Serpentine Drive in the heart of Spartanburg County, the employee-owned, acute-care medical/surgical hospital offers a range of services and specialties.

Nationally recognized for its treatment of kidney stones,

only such center of its kind in the area, where eye specialists provide highly effective solutions to eye problems that are less painful than traditional treatment methods. Because of its small size and friendly atmosphere, Doctors Memorial is also the hospital of choice for many same-day surgery procedures and outpatient services such as physical and occupational therapy. An 11-bed, skilled-care unit provides short-term care for patients during the transition period after an acute illness.

The hospital recently received accreditation with commendation from JCAHO, an accomplishment shared with less than 5 percent of American hospitals.

MARY BLACK MEMORIAL HOSPITAL

Mary Black Memorial Hospital is Spartanburg's only private, not-for-profit hospital. The original 35-bed facility was established in 1925 by Dr. Hugh Ratchford Black in honor of his wife, Mary Snoddy Black. Today, the hospital has 208 acute-care beds at its main campus at 1700 Skylyn Drive, three miles east of downtown Spartanburg. The hospital established the Mary Black Westside Medical Park at 2995

Mary Black's Emergency Department is open 24 hours a day, year-round.

With a strong commitment to community education, Mary Black offers programs on a wide variety of health care topics each month at the hospital and on-site at area offices and businesses.

SPARTANBURG REGIONAL MEDICAL CENTER

Opened in 1921, Spartanburg Regional Medical Center is now a

inpatient unit, a spacious and attractive outpatient treatment center, a full range of chemotherapy and other treatments, and the latest in radiation therapy, including a computerized treatment simulator and linear accelerators.

The Level I Trauma Center at Spartanburg Regional provides the highest level of emergency care 24 hours a day. Surgical suites operate around the clock, using lasers, laparoscopes, and innovative orthopedic surgery.

Reidville to serve the citizens on the growing west side of Spartanburg. Providing specialized services such as urgent care, women's health care, and industrial medicine, the medical park also is home to several private specialty physicians.

Mary Black Memorial Hospital is equipped and staffed to handle complex medical problems. Among its specialty areas are women's health, orthopedics, inpatient and outpatient surgery, oncology, and pediatrics. Its 18-bed Center for Rehabilitative Medicine is the only total-care rehabilitation unit in Spartanburg County. The hospital also is renowned for the care provided by its Family Birthing Center, where childbirth is a family affair with most procedures performed in one comfortable room, supported by the latest technology.

588-bed, comprehensive diagnostic and treatment center serving five counties in Upstate South Carolina and western North Carolina. With more than 300 physicians and dentists on staff, the hospital cares for more than 140,000 patients each year.

The Heart Center at Spartanburg Regional, with 96 private rooms, is an anchor hospital for Emergency Heart Network, a group of community hospitals with specially trained staff to treat heart attacks as they are occurring. The state-of-the-art facility performs more than 300 open-heart surgeries and approximately 2,500 heart catheterizations annually.

Comprehensive cancer diagnosis and treatment is another specialty at Spartanburg Regional. Cancer services include a 30-bed

The Center for Women is another center of excellence at Spartanburg Regional, with 33 private rooms for maternity and medical/surgical care. The Center for Women also includes a Neonatal Intensive Care Unit equipped with the most sophisticated life-support systems to care for the smallest or sickest newborns.

A Family Resource Center offers seminars and community wellness programs in the Center for Women. Other wellness programs such as seminars, mammograms, and health screenings are taken out to businesses, schools, and civic groups in Spartanburg and surrounding counties.

Fluor Daniel

Among Fluor Daniel's Spartanburg County projects are (clockwise from above) the headquarters tower for Flagstar Companies, Inc., an expansion at the Greenville-Spartanburg Airport, BMW's first American production facility, and Milliken & Company's customer service center.

FLUOR DANIEL, WITH A MAJOR OFFICE IN GREENVILLE, SOUTH CAROLINA, SERVES MORE clients in more industries in more locations than any other company that provides engineering, construction, maintenance, and related technical services. Fluor Daniel is becoming particularly prominent in Spartanburg County as general contractor for the first American plant built for BMW, the German luxury automaker. ◆ From more than 50 offices and operations around the world, Fluor Daniel has tackled a

range of projects, from one-person assignments to jobs requiring thousands of engineers, specialists, and craftworkers. With broad market diversity and an emphasis on value-added services, Fluor Daniel assists clients in attaining a competitive advantage by delivering quality services of unmatched value. The company emphasizes meticulous attention to detail in every job, large or small, and its safety record is one of the best among contractors worldwide.

Although its origins go back more than 80 years, Fluor Daniel was created as a new company in 1986 by combining the strengths of two of the world's most prestigious organizations in engineering and construction, Fluor Corporation and Daniel International. Daniel International was founded in 1934 in Anderson, South Carolina, under the name Daniel Construction Company. The company moved to Greenville in 1942. Fluor Corporation was established in Santa Ana, California, in 1912.

The company performs engineering, construction, and maintenance services for a range of sophisticated processes, products, and industries, including biotechnology, chemicals and plastics, electronics, power, and pharmaceuticals. Fluor Daniel also has a long-standing reputation in food and beverages, mining and metals, pulp and paper, petroleum, petrochemicals, and pipelines. In addition, it serves the telecommunications, transportation, and space and defense industries, and provides environmental services to a broad range of industries.

Fluor Daniel projects are among the most prestigious in the area. They include the Greenville-Spartanburg Airport, the 17-story TW Services (now Flagstar) tower

in downtown Spartanburg, the Milliken & Company campus and manufacturing facilities, and the MEMC Electronics Materials, Inc. building.

In support of the local community, Fluor Daniel representatives serve on the board of directors of Converse College. The company is also a member of the Spartanburg Area Chamber of Commerce.

DEDICATED TO CLIENT SATISFACTION

The company considers client satisfaction paramount, and its client relationships continue to grow and strengthen due to Fluor Daniel's total service approach. Those relationships often become global in scope as many clients internationalize their operations. Fluor Daniel

has alliances with more than 30 companies in which it serves as an extension of a client's organization, participating in such activities as the capital planning process. Fluor Daniel people take pride in the fact that a remarkable 78 percent of the company's business is from clients they have previously served.

To achieve the highest level of client satisfaction, Fluor Daniel employs a philosophy called Con-

STEVE FINCHER

tinuous Performance Improvement, which pervades every job that every employee performs. This philosophy creates an atmosphere of innovation in which people are encouraged to work in teams and are recognized for their responsiveness to client needs.

Fluor Daniel's global network of talented people, international experience, and financial strength will continue to provide clients with true value and excellence.

Mayfair Mills, Inc.

WHILE THE TEXTILE INDUSTRY IN THE UNITED STATES HAS UNDERGONE TREMENdous downsizing, mergers, and acquisitions in recent years, Mayfair Mills, founded in Spartanburg in 1934, has remained a constant. In fact, if you ask Chairman of the Board Frederick B. Dent about the company's greatest accomplishment, his answer is unequivocal: "Growing and staying alive." ◆ "To have modernized our plants, to have expanded, to have given our people

steady income with profit sharing so that they can have stable family lives—this is a testament to the quality of our associates, our suppliers, and particularly our customers," he says. "We have never had a layoff."

Mayfair Mills has accomplished this in part by involving every associate in quality improvement. In 1980 the company started studying the concepts of Total Quality Management developed by W. Edwards Deming and then trained some of its personnel in this field at George Washington University. Mayfair Mills was one of the first to join the Quality in the Workplace program of the Spartanburg Area Chamber of Commerce when it began in 1984.

Although the company has a formal quality improvement program in place today, parts of it have been practiced at Mayfair Mills for decades. For example, associates have worked in teams since the 1960s, long before the concept came into vogue. "It continues to be one of our greatest sources of improvement," Dent explains. "We bring a lot of people into decision-making and give them the tools to make good decisions. Our people are very competent and by far our greatest asset." The company spends more than $1 million annually on education and training.

QUALITY PRODUCTS AND FACILITIES

Mayfair Mills is a weaver of premium quality unbleached and undyed cloth ("greige" goods) for purchase by other companies that turn them into finished products such as men's and ladies' apparel,

home furnishings and decorative items, and industrial fabrics. Mayfair's products are sold exclusively by Joshua L. Baily & Co., Inc. of Hoboken, New Jersey.

Employing 2,000 associates in six plants in South Carolina and Georgia, Mayfair Mills also has remained competitive by continually investing in the most modern equipment. Computerized instruments monitor the fiber selection process as well as each stage of fabric development.

"Our unswerving focus has been on satisfying the customer," says Frederick B. Dent Jr., company president. "We are constantly striving to learn what the customer wants so that we can meet expectations in terms of product quality, delivery, and price."

COMMUNITY AND INDUSTRY INVOLVEMENT

Mayfair Mills has been actively involved in nearly every aspect of

the community, including business development, education, medical services, law enforcement, and government.

The company also is active in state and national trade associations, providing leadership and support. Mayfair Mills was one of the founding members of the Crafted with Pride in the U.S.A. Council, Inc., which promotes the purchase of American textile products. It also recently earned a place in the "Encouraging Environmental Excellence" program of the American Textile Manufacturers Institute, Inc. by meeting a rigorous set of environmental standards.

Says President Dent, "We are committed to our customers. We are committed to our associates. We are committed to being an example for our industry and a contributor to improving the quality of life in our community."

A quality team inspects cloth at one of Mayfair's six plants in South Carolina and Georgia (above).

The company has remained competitive by continually investing in the most modern equipment, like these high-tech, open-end spinning frames (left).

Mayfair Mills is today led by Chairman of the Board Frederick B. Dent (left) and President Frederick B. Dent Jr.

JM Smith Corporation

T HE HISTORY OF JM SMITH CORPORATION BRINGS TO MIND TWO VERY DIFFERENT images. The first is a Norman Rockwell-style portrait of the family pharmacist, mortar and pestle in hand, surrounded by corked bottles on rows of overstuffed shelves. He chats with his customers as he mixes the elixirs of recovery, and he knows everyone's children by name. The second image is a snapshot of an electronics aficionado who is working intently in an unadorned office cubicle. Unaware

of his surroundings, he is tapping codes into a computer keyboard to develop a new software program.

It's hard to put the two images together and find them working compatibly, much less forming the basis of one of South Carolina's top 20 privately held corporations. Yet the blending of the two fields— pharmacy and computer science— along with a long-standing commitment to customer service and innovation, is the foundation for what is now a $150-million business. Comprising Spartanburg-based JM Smith Corporation are Smith Drug Company, Smith Data Processing, and QS/1 Data Systems.

THE SMITH FAMILY LEGACY
The story begins with a man named James M. Smith, who opened a pharmacy in Asheville, North Carolina, in 1925. He then began establishing pharmacies in other locales, bringing in partners for the individual stores to ensure that each one was independent and could operate as its owners saw fit. By the late 1930s, the list included 17 pharmacies throughout the Carolinas and Georgia. Smith visited each store every week to ensure quality.

By 1940 Smith saw that the pharmacies would benefit from a warehouse for joint purchasing. Several years later Smith sold his interest in all of the stores to establish Smith Drug Company in Spartanburg.

His two sons, Jim and Henry Dale, both registered pharmacists, were as energetic and enterprising as their father. When the elder

Smith died in 1951, Jim and Henry Dale took the reins of the Spartanburg company. The brothers then followed their father's plans and established another pharmaceutical company (not a part of JM Smith Corp.) in Springfield, Illinois, which Henry Dale headed up.

James Smith Jr. (Jim) had graduated third in his class at age 19 from the Massachusetts Institute of Technology with a degree in electrical engineering. He later received a degree in pharmacy from the University of South Carolina. It was his mastery of these disparate disciplines that led to the company's expansion into data processing and computer services. He computerized Smith Drug Company in 1959 and a few years later established Smith Data Processing (SDP). An outgrowth of SDP was QS/1 Data Systems, which became a separate operating division in 1990.

Jim led the growth of JM Smith Corporation until his own death in 1985. At that time Henry Dale became chairman and CEO, the positions he holds today. Jim and Henry Dale were ably

assisted in that growth by Bill Shelley, former president of the drug division who retired in 1992, and Glenn Hammett, former president of the data processing division who retired in 1991.

Henry Dale feels that a family business like JM Smith can achieve

the greatest strength by turning over its leadership and continuing to progress. Building on the foundation in place, the company has seen its data processing revenue more than double, its wholesale drug revenue more than triple, and its net worth more than quadruple in the past seven years.

JM Smith is composed of three distinct companies, yet they operate compatibly under the four premises set forth by the Smith family. According to Ken Couch, presi-

From its corporate headquarters in Spartanburg (right), JM Smith operates three companies—Smith Data Processing, Smith Drug Company, and QS/1 Data Systems—which combine to form a $150-million corporation.

From a modest beginning in a small pharmacy in Asheville, North Carolina, J.M. Smith (above) set trends that community pharmacies and the pharmaceutical industry have followed for decades.

dent of Smith Drug Company, they are: "Take care of your customers, and they'll take care of you. Take care of your employees, and they'll take care of business. Be careful with your finances. And be a good and gracious corporate citizen."

SMITH DRUG COMPANY

While opening his office mail one morning, Ken Couch enjoyed the comments of a long-standing customer. In his letter, the customer said he couldn't imagine running a pharmacy without the prompt attention and quick service of Smith Drug Company. But he added a word of caution: "Don't ever lose your personal touch."

Indeed, that personal touch is the hallmark of the company as well as its customers. Smith Drug

supplies independent, locally owned pharmacies in the Carolinas with everything from shampoo to the most sophisticated cancer treatment drugs.

One of only 70 wholesale drug companies in the United States, Smith Drug brings in more than 75 percent of JM Smith Corporation's gross revenue. In addition to community pharmacies, the company serves all major hospitals in the region and a growing number of college and university health centers.

"We operate under the prime vendor programs, serving independent and institutional pharmacies exclusively," says Couch. "We understand the market pressures on the independent community phar-

macy, and we want to be part of their success. We want that pharmacist to pick up the phone or, increasingly, communicate with us via computer to order everything from Smith Drug."

To meet these expectations, the company purchases more than 31,000 products from 400 or more suppliers to carry everything from wheelchairs to biotech drugs. The latest addition to the warehouse facility, completed in 1988, is already bursting at the seams, and there are plans to expand.

Smith Drug's business is growing despite a shrinking market. Nationwide, the number of independent pharmacies decreased from 36,000 to 30,000 over a 12-year period from 1981 to 1993, and another third will be gone by the turn of the century, Couch estimates. But Smith Drug outperforms its competition in terms of delivery and service, so the company anticipates continued growth.

Some aspects of the business are state-of-the-art. For example, Smith Drug provides bar code labels for community and hospital pharmacies and provides hand-held computers to link them directly with the warehouse. Pharmaceutical areas in the company warehouse are continuously monitored for temperature and humidity levels to assure product integrity. The

One of only 70 wholesale drug companies in the United States, Smith Drug represents more than 75 percent of JM Smith's gross revenue, and services community pharmacies and hospitals throughout South Carolina and western North Carolina.

Smith Data Processing is the premier supplier of data processing services to local governments in South Carolina. Hundreds of cities, counties, and schools turn to SDP for all or part of their data processing services.

QS/1's headquarters (right) for U.S. and Canadian operations is located in Spartanburg.

computer area, where incoming orders are received, checked, and invoiced, is a flurry of blinking screens and printouts.

Other aspects are more down-to-earth. Orders are repacked in cartons received from the company's suppliers, many times with the polystyrene "peanuts" that came with them or with newspaper that employees bring from home. These and other measures help keep costs down while highlighting environmental awareness. Anyone not involved in filling an order helps with housekeeping to keep the warehouse immaculate. The company's 107 employees are eager to pitch in because many own company stock; in fact, only employees are allowed to purchase stock in the closely held company.

SMITH DATA PROCESSING

"My brother was a brilliant man," says Henry Dale Smith. "In the 1950s he foresaw what computers could do for the wholesale drug business and retail pharmacies. When Jim began computerizing Smith Drug Company, he made sure we had excess computing capacity to tinker, experiment, and innovate. He knew there was a tremendous opportunity to fill the

needs of others by doing processing work."

Today, Smith Data Processing, which James Smith Jr. founded in 1959, is the premier supplier of data processing services and systems to local government agencies in South Carolina. In the early days, the business consisted of batch processing services for government and businesses. Today, the division still processes millions of tax notices, payroll records, inventories, and even school report cards through its mainframe computers.

In the early 1970s, SDP saw that local governments needed computer systems that could process data in-house. Addressing that need led to what has become the

division's primary product—software for in-office systems that help manage law enforcement departments, judicial offices, municipal utilities, city and county billings and collections, financial departments, and other local government activities. Currently, more than 500 local government agencies in South Carolina process daily records with SDP systems.

Additionally, SDP processes prescription claims for preferred provider organizations and has its own prescription card program. Known as the Premier Pharmacy Plan, the program is a national prescription drug program designed to effectively manage and control prescription drug benefits.

SDP also provides data processing forms and supplies primarily to pharmacy and dental customers of sister division QS/1 Data Systems. Through this fast-growing area, SDP helps design forms that help customers meet changing government regulations and industry standards.

"Accuracy, dependability, and fast response are what customers want, and we work very hard to provide that to them," says SDP President A.W. Smith, who is of no relation to the founding family. "We work very hard to anticipate their needs and stay on top of industry trends and changing regulations. We know that, more than anything else, quality service and support are why we continue to grow year after year. And that's where our efforts go."

QS/1 Data Systems

When work began 16 years ago to develop a computer system to help pharmacists manage their practices, no one knew those efforts were creating what would become the number one computer system among independent pharmacies in North America. Called the QS/1

government regulations, and even print labels for medicine vials.

Today, QS/1 Pharmacy Systems are used in approximately 6,000 independent pharmacies in the United States and Canada—about twice as many as the closest competitor. While the system is recognized as the most comprehensive in the industry, the real reason behind its astounding success is a dedication to customer service:

minute they are open. We owe it to them to keep them at the forefront of health care and to be there when they need us. We meet with customers regularly to see how we can serve them better, and we use those meetings as a blueprint for better service."

A national toll-free service center fields calls daily from customers. Additionally, QS/1 has nine offices strategically located

More community pharmacies across the country rely on the QS/1 Pharmacy System than any other system available today.

Pharmacy System (named for the pharmacy term "quantum sufficient," meaning "to fill as needed," and the IBM Series/1 computer for which the software was originally designed), it helped pharmacists maintain customer records, manage reams of paperwork required by

QS/1's very first customer is still with the company 16 years later.

"We work very hard to keep our customers," says William R. Cobb, president of QS/1 Data Systems. "By using our system, they have put a lot of trust in us because they depend on our system every

throughout North America to support customers.

Keeping an ear finely tuned to customer needs has also led to additional product development, including a system to manage sales and rental of home medical equipment, a point-of-sale system that manages the front-end or non-prescription section of a pharmacy through a computerized cash register, an electronic claims switching service that processes an average of 2.5 million prescription insurance claims each month, and a patient counseling service that enables a pharmacist to provide patients with a detailed monograph concerning a prescription.

Development and support of all QS/1 services are handled by the company's own team of highly skilled staff, most of whom are headquartered in the Spartanburg offices.

Blue Cross and Blue Shield of South Carolina

FOR ALMOST 50 YEARS, BLUE CROSS AND BLUE SHIELD OF SOUTH CAROLINA HAS BEEN A symbol of hope and security for the Upstate. As the state's largest health insurer, the company covers more South Carolina residents than the next 16 leading health insurers combined. Statewide, more than 780,000 employees and individuals depend on Blue Cross and Blue Shield for insurance protection. ◆ In Spartanburg County, thousands of citizens are insured by the company through corporate and personal

coverage. These individuals also enjoy the Preferred Personal Care plan offered through the community's two largest hospitals and a number of local physicians.

SERVING THE UPSTATE SINCE 1946

Blue Cross of South Carolina first opened in nearby Greenville in 1946 with fewer than eight employees. In 1957 the company moved its home offices to Columbia, a more central location that allowed Blue Cross to better serve

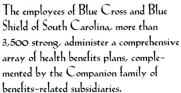
The employees of Blue Cross and Blue Shield of South Carolina, more than 3,500 strong, administer a comprehensive array of health benefits plans, complemented by the Companion family of benefits-related subsidiaries.

its growing list of clients and to operate more efficiently statewide.

With a current work force of more than 3,500, Blue Cross has satellite offices in Greenville, Charleston, Florence, and Camden. The company serves Spartanburg through these area offices and its 12-story headquarters complex at Interstate 20 and Alpine Road in Columbia.

Blue Cross is the parent company of a family of benefits-related subsidiaries, which enable the company to serve an array of client needs. Companion HealthCare is the company's health maintenance organization, while Companion Life offers life, disability, and other insurance products. Companion Property and Casualty sells workers' compensation, liability, and other business insurance. Companion Capital Management provides financial management and investment services, and Companion

Technologies markets and services computer hardware and software. Through the comprehensive network of Companion companies, Blue Cross coordinates services and products that enhance and complement its health benefits plans.

Blue Cross is also a major government contractor. The company has administered Medicare for the federal government throughout

South Carolina since the program's inception in 1966. In 1991 Blue Cross began processing claims for the federal- and state-funded Medicaid program. As the nation's largest CHAMPUS (Civilian Health and Medical Program for the Uniformed Services) contractor, Blue Cross provides medical coverage for military dependents and retirees worldwide.

AN INNOVATOR IN HEALTH CARE

Meeting the constantly changing needs of the health care consumer means that Blue Cross is more than a health insurance company. The corporation closely monitors market changes and constantly updates its products and services to meet new challenges. New services consistently reflect trends in cost savings and health care management. According to Blue Cross management, the company's ability to anticipate and analyze change in the health care industry has allowed Blue Cross to offer innovative approaches to the changing marketplace.

"Consumers are taking a keen interest in health care and health care planning in the '90s," says President and CEO Ed Sellers. "Upon examination, they'll find that Blue Cross and Blue Shield provides a timely selection of services to meet a variety of needs. Whenever South Carolinians need us, we'll be here—today, tomorrow, or in the years to come."

Spartan Radiocasting Company

T HE SPARTAN RADIOCASTING COMPANY, OWNER OF AWARD-WINNING CBS NETWORK affiliate WSPA-TV and radio stations WSPA-AM and WSPA-FM, has been a leader in the area's broadcasting community for almost 50 years. From its state-of-the-art studios and offices at Communications Park in Spartanburg, SRC produces high-quality programming and comprehensive news coverage, and offers the area's finest commercial production facilities.

The Spartan Radiocasting Company is synonymous with Walter J. Brown, who founded the company and today serves as chairman and chief executive officer.

Brown, with a distinguished career in journalism launched in Washington, D.C., moved to Spartanburg in 1940 to serve as general manager of the Spartanburg Advertising Company. During World War II he was called to return to Washington to serve as special assistant to James F. Byrnes, before and during Byrnes' term as Secretary of State.

Following the war, in 1947, Brown founded SRC and purchased WSPA-AM, the oldest commercial radio station in the state. Founded in 1930, the station has been affiliated with the CBS Radio Network since 1943. In 1947 SRC also purchased WSPA-FM, which was established the year before as South Carolina's first FM station. WSPA-FM today broadcasts "Lite Contemporary Adult Music" to 94 counties in South Carolina, North Carolina, and Georgia.

Also in 1947, Brown began a prolonged and herculean effort to establish a television station on Channel 7 in Spartanburg. He prevailed in a four-year court battle over the site of the new station (the channel was originally assigned to another South Carolina city), and WSPA-TV finally went on the air on April 29, 1956.

SRC also owns and operates WJBF-TV in Augusta, Georgia; WBTW-TV in Florence, South Carolina; KMIT-TV in Mason City, Iowa; and WMBB-TV in Panama City, Florida.

SRC TODAY

Today, WSPA-TV is the top-rated TV station in viewership in its market, which serves almost 2 million people in South Carolina, North Carolina, and Georgia. One of the few locally owned and operated stations in the nation, it is also one of the best equipped and staffed. Its cutting-edge production facilities are used by area professionals to produce commercials, training films, and a variety of promotional pieces.

The two radio stations and WSPA-TV provide outstanding news coverage and entertainment, and produce a wealth of programs about important issues, the people, and special events in the communities they serve. Since its beginning, SRC has provided leadership for innumerable civic, charitable, and cultural efforts to improve life for all citizens of Spartanburg.

The company's commitment to broadcasting excellence and to the welfare of the Spartanburg community is reflected in the numerous awards presented to both SRC and Walter Brown. WSPA-TV was named Station of the Year by the South Carolina Broadcaster's Association (SCBA) in 1989 and has won SCBA's Best Children's Programming award seven times. Likewise, Walter Brown was named to the South Carolina Broadcasters Hall of Fame in 1975, and in 1990 the Walter J. Brown Briefing Center was dedicated at the new headquarters office of the Spartanburg Area Chamber of Commerce.

SRC is synonymous with Walter J. Brown (left), who founded the company and today serves as chairman and chief executive officer.

As the company approaches its 50th anniversary in 1997, Brown and Spartan Radiocasting Company remain committed to providing the best news, programming, and community support in Spartanburg and beyond.

From its state-of-the-art studios and offices, Spartan Radiocasting Company produces high-quality programming and comprehensive news coverage.

Roebuck Buildings Co., Inc.

ROEBUCK BUILDINGS CO., INC. HAS EVOLVED IN THE 1990S FROM A COMPANY SPECIALIZing solely in pre-engineered metal buildings to a premier general contractor in Spartanburg County. The Roebuck Buildings logo today graces a variety of construction sites—from multistory office complexes and upscale retail stores to simple metal warehouses. Among the company's recent projects are Holly Hall at the Carolina Country Club, downtown Spartanburg's Broadwalk office and retail complex, the

Travers Tool building at the elegant SpartanGreen industrial park at I-85 and Highway 290, and the Greenville County Recreational Facility featuring indoor tennis courts and ice-skating facilities.

PROSPERING AND CHANGING WITH THE TIMES

In 1947 when John C. Anderson, then a commercial credit officer for a bank, and a group of investors started Roebuck Buildings, the preengineered building industry was in its infancy. As the market matured, the company prospered. During the 1950s, Roebuck constructed

warehouses and large retail buildings, such as car dealerships, in a geographic area ranging from Virginia to Florida.

Roebuck Buildings began its transformation to a full-service contractor in the mid-1980s. Like many other construction companies at that time, Roebuck found itself at a crossroads due to the tightening of the building market. The company's particular dilemma was that it had grown too large to compete with the smaller firms in the prefabricated building market, and it was too small to compete with the larger companies for more complex projects. At the same time Roebuck had already embarked on a course of change: John Anderson was planning his retirement, and his son, Dean, would soon become company president and CEO.

"We had to make a decision whether to scale back or grow," says Dean Anderson, reflecting on

that period. "We chose the latter and decided to expand into a completely different kind of company." To accomplish that, Roebuck Buildings began computerizing its operations and developing computer-aided design capabilities. Then, another medium-size general contracting company in Spartanburg closed. Says Anderson, "We snatched the cream of the crop of their people, which gave us more expertise in general construction."

Today, the company offers the full range of contracting services and excels in turnkey projects. Roebuck serves clients in North Carolina, Tennessee, and Georgia, as well as South Carolina. The company also is involved to a limited degree in development, but only in areas where it will not compete with clients who are developers.

The company's headquarters is in Roebuck, five miles south of

Among the company's recent projects are the Travers Tool building (right) at SpartanGreen industrial park and Milliken's Sharon plant in Abbeville, South Carolina (above).

Roebuck Buildings has also constructed the Broadwalk office and retail complex in downtown Spartanburg (left) and Holly Hall at the Carolina Country Club (below).

Spartanburg along Highway 221. John Anderson established it there because his family owned peach orchards nearby. Although the Andersons no longer farm, Roebuck Buildings remains a family business. Dean Anderson's brother-in-law, William G. Sarratt, serves as vice president of marketing for the company.

A QUALITY OPERATION

The business has thrived through conscientious attention to detail and by offering its customers the highest quality construction at the lowest cost possible. "Our expertise is in value-engineering, which means working with the client from the very beginning of a project, sharing our ideas on design and cost benefits," Dean Anderson says. He adds that Roebuck personnel are the most important resource he has to offer clients: Many of them have worked with the company since its beginning, and others have as many as 30 years of experience in the construction business.

Constantly working to refine its capabilities, Roebuck Buildings has adopted Total Quality Management (TQM) as a policy that will yield long-term benefits for both the company and its clients. "It's an entirely different way of doing business, and we are committed to making the most of it," Anderson says. The company's consistently improving safety record also is a point of pride for Roebuck Buildings. Its superior performance has in fact made for many satisfied customers: more than 50 percent of the company's revenue is derived from repeat clients.

As might be expected from an industry leader, Roebuck Buildings is also a community leader through its involvement in many civic, educational, and charitable endeavors. The company, which has long supported organizations that help young people with disabilities, recently built at cost a multipurpose recreational building for the South Carolina School for the Deaf and the Blind and also helped finance the building. An effort organized by the Civitan Club and the Foundation for the Multi-handicapped, the building is providing a highly appreciated arena for helping multi-handicapped individuals reach their potential.

With its resources and capabilities in place and its direction set, Roebuck Buildings is prepared for the 1990s and beyond. "We want to continue to be Spartanburg's leading general contractor," says Anderson. "We have the personnel and the financial strength to be a long-term player providing high-quality workmanship and customer satisfaction."

McAbee, Talbert, Halliday & Co.

McABEE, TALBERT, HALLIDAY & CO. IS A MEDIUM-SIZE ACCOUNTING AND CONSULTing firm that doesn't act like one. In many ways, it behaves more like a large national firm, providing specialties and services beyond what clients expect. Yet it adheres to the small-practice philosophy of personalized service and value. ◆ The largest and most diverse independent accounting organization in the Spartanburg area, McAbee, Talbert, Halliday & Co. is a firm of specialties, not partners.

Each of its directors brings focused talents to its range of services, from implementing computerized accounting systems, to designing employee benefit plans, to conducting sophisticated audits.

The company began in 1952 as a partnership between Robert Gilman and Boyce Brannon. As the firm grew, other young CPAs became partners, and the founders retired. In July of 1987 the company adopted its current management structure and became known as McAbee, Talbert, Halliday & Co. With 30 employees and 8,000 square feet of office space on East Main Street, the firm is led by directors Homer E. McAbee Jr., Charles L. Talbert III, Q. Stanford Halliday III, Randolph B. Thomas, and Bruce W. Schwartz.

AREAS OF GROWTH AND EXPERTISE

Small-business development has been one area of growth for the firm. Emerging companies often lack the expertise to perform their own accounting functions, yet they recognize the need to develop sound policies and procedures from the start. McAbee, Talbert, Halliday & Co. stands ready with business and management consulting services to help move young businesses toward self-sufficient systems and to assist established businesses with existing systems. The firm has invested in a state-of-the-art computer network, which provides the firm's staff with the necessary training and tools to perform such services.

For many clients, taxation expertise is the most important aspect of their relationship with the firm.

Planning for tax-wise strategies through extensive tax law research is a primary strength of McAbee, Talbert, Halliday & Co., which maintains one of the most comprehensive tax libraries in the area. By continually monitoring rulings of the courts and the Internal Revenue Service, the firm keeps abreast of the complex and ever-changing tax structure.

McAbee, Talbert, Halliday & Co. is also highly respected in the areas of auditing and accounting. The firm believes that a financial statement should be more than a compliance document for lenders; it should be a reliable tool with which to make informed decisions. In fact, the audit and accounting practice undergoes regular peer review to provide independent assurance of quality.

With active membership in the American Institute of Certified Public Accountants (including both the Private Companies Practice Section and the Securities and

Exchange Commission Practice Section) and the CPA associations in North and South Carolina, the firm helps ensure improved standards industrywide and within its own practice. Through its membership in the National Associated CPA Firms, McAbee, Talbert, Halliday & Co. can offer comprehensive accounting and consulting services to domestic and interna-

tional companies. Among its current clients are firms importing from or exporting to Europe, Central and South America, and the Pacific Rim.

With a history of low client turnover and a practice growing with the region, McAbee, Talbert, Halliday & Co. does more than simply make the numbers add up. For more than four decades, this Spartanburg firm has strived to offer the expertise of a national accounting organization with the personalized service of a home-grown company.

The directors and staff of McAbee, Talbert, Halliday & Co. are committed to providing the expertise of a large national firm with the personal attention of a small, hometown practice.

OLENCKI GRAPHICS

Brian Lyttle, Inc.

I N 1947, 12 YEARS BEFORE MOVING FROM IRELAND TO THE UNITED STATES TO OPEN SPARTAN-burg County's first European textile equipment sales office, Brian Mackey Lyttle learned firsthand what it means to be a survivor. The call was so close he even has a copy of his own obituary. ◆ An aeronautical engineer by training, Captain Lyttle was flying a test plane across the Irish Sea without instrumentation when the engines failed and the plane plunged into the frigid waters. He floated on a wing segment for more than 12

hours until the captain of a potato boat discovered him by "sensing" him through the mist. The boat had no radio and a strict delivery schedule along the Irish coast to keep, so it was four days before Captain Lyttle could notify his family that he was alive and well. He arrived home just in time to read his obituary in a Belfast newspaper.

"We laugh about it now, but he'll be the first to tell you it makes you realize how important every moment is," says his son, Peter I.M. Lyttle, who today serves as president of Brian Lyttle, Inc.

THE COMPANY'S STORY

The company's story is also one of survival. In Spartanburg in 1959, Brian Lyttle opened Hobourn Sales, a division of Hobourn Aero Components of Rochester, England. The division's purpose was to provide sales and service of Agilon machinery, which texturized yarn for hosiery. By the early 1960s, the market was saturated and Hobourn made plans to close its American operation. Instead, Brian bought the company in 1964, changed the name to Brian Lyttle, Inc., and developed relationships with other manufacturers.

In the last half of the 1960s, Brian Lyttle, Inc. introduced three new products to the U.S. textile industry: machines for the production of double-knit fabrics that were immensely popular in the 1960s and 1970s, sublimation printing machinery for printing on double-knit and other polyester fabrics, and automatic toe-closing

machinery for the ladies' hosiery industry.

When double-knit fabrics went out of style almost overnight in the 1970s, the company found itself not only without a major product line, but also facing a

downturn in the textile industry. Brian Lyttle, Inc. has survived and regained its footing by diversifying into supplying screen-printers with inks and equipment, and by developing new products unrelated to textiles.

"Over the years, Dad has had the vision and the foresight to take four products in the textile industry from idea to market development to market saturation. Now he's doing it again in another industry," Peter Lyttle says.

While Peter has kept the company growing by supplying close to 1,000 screen-printing businesses, his father has been developing a new product—a chemical-free water purification system for swimming pools and hot tubs. Initial

production is under way at the company's 22,000-square-foot facility facing I-85, just north of Highway 221. The company also is developing sales of fiber-optic lighting systems and acrylic building blocks for the consumer market.

"Dad has a favorite saying: 'Never say something can't be done.' If you work smart enough and give it your best, anything is possible. This will be his legacy," Peter Lyttle says.

In 1959 Brian Mackey Lyttle opened Spartanburg County's first European textile equipment sales office. Today, his resilient company is diversifying within the industry and developing new products unrelated to textiles.

Prym-Dritz Corporation

TODAY'S "CREATIVE CONSUMER" DEPENDS ON THE PRYM-DRITZ CORPORATION, ONE OF the world's largest manufacturers and suppliers of sewing and craft notions. "We regard the consumer of our products to be the home crafter. This includes the home sewer, who makes and repairs clothing and home decorating accessories, as well as the crafter, who turns quilting and machine embroidery into an art form," says President Paul N. Mackey. ◆ Creative consumers insist on quality in their

As a natural extension of its slogan— Excellence Through Teamwork—Prym-Dritz strives to foster a family-like work atmosphere with open communication among its employees (right).

sewing notions and craft products, which range from pins and needles to measuring tools and fabric dyes. By consistently rising to the high standards of home crafters nation-

All U.S. Prym operations were centralized to Spartanburg in 1990. The sprawling complex houses the most technologically advanced manufacturing, warehousing, packaging, and shipping operation in one highly efficient 220,000-square-foot facility (above).

wide, Prym-Dritz has grown by almost 100 employees in the past five years and increased its sales from $27 million to $46 million during that period. "This growth did not result from growth of the market, but from our own market penetration and the expansion of our range of products," Mackey explains.

The company's tag line, "America's Notion Company," is no exaggeration; in fact, Prym-Dritz is the largest manufacturer and distributor of sewing notions in the country. In all 50 states, Prym-Dritz serves both independent and chain fabric stores, as well as the sewing and craft departments of leading variety and discount stores. In addition, about 20 percent of its products are sold to the industrial trade, such as dry cleaners and apparel manufacturers.

A DIVERSITY OF PRODUCTS

Items produced or distributed by the company include sewing tools; machine accessories; thread organizers and kits; marking, measuring, and cutting equipment; pressing equipment; dressforms; buttons, buckles, and belts to cover; and repair and replacement items, such as iron-on patches and trouser repair pockets. Prym-Dritz manufactures most of its own metal goods, such as straight pins, safety pins, snaps, hooks and eyes, and covered buttons.

Quilting is one of the fastest growing crafts in the United States. "The Quiltery" by Prym-Dritz includes all the basic tools a quilter needs, ranging from quilting pins and needles to marking tools and special quilting rulers. The company also offers rotary cutters and mats for cutting intricate patchwork designs. For the novice quilter, there are patchwork template sets with step-by-step instructions for making well-known patterns, such as the Ohio Star and the Bear's Paw.

Responding to the growing interest in home decorating, Prym-Dritz offers a full line of sew-in and iron-on drapery tapes and accessories, along with tools, tacks, and supplies for upholstering furniture. The company also provides assistance to the retailer with a point-of-purchase video designed to attract attention to the iron-on tapes and an instructional video that gives the consumer ideas for using the tapes, as well as tips for applying them.

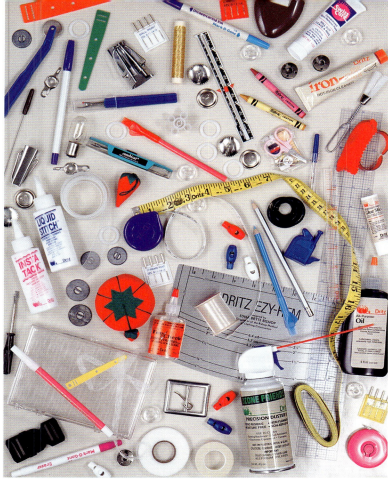

"We have almost saturated the market in the traditional fabric store area," Mackey says, adding that Prym-Dritz plans to further diversify its mix of products for the home crafter and to increase its sensitivity to the needs and tastes of customers. "We will make every effort to introduce more new and innovative products, with the goal of solving problems and meeting new fashion, craft, and home decorating requirements."

As part of that mission, Prym-Dritz has attained exclusive distributorship rights for Dylon fabric and craft dyes produced in England. Other Dylon fabric care products include Run Away, which removes color runs from washable white fabrics; Color Shield, which sets colors on non-colorfast fabrics; Double Duty, a fabric whitener and stain remover; and Simply White, which returns whiteness to lace, net, and sheer curtains.

"Many of our products are made right here in the Spartanburg plant," says Mackey. "One of our great strengths is the assurance that they are manufactured to exceptionally high quality standards. We understand our customers and know that something as simple as a dull pin can frustrate an otherwise enjoyable project."

GROWTH AND CHANGE SINCE 1960

Spartanburg's Prym-Dritz operation first opened in 1960 as a packaging facility for the Scovill notion company, established by John Dritz in the 1940s. In 1980 it was purchased by Risdon, a worldwide wire manufacturer. Management acquired the company through a buyout in 1985, then sold it in 1988 to the Prym Company of Stolberg, Germany, which had also purchased the Connecticut-based Dritz Corporation (formerly Scovill). With 4,500 employees worldwide, the family-owned Prym Company, founded over 400 years ago, is the largest manufacturer of straight pins and safety pins in the world.

All U.S. Prym operations were centralized to Spartanburg in 1990, and the manufacturing facility was expanded with a 42,000-square-foot addition. The sprawling complex, facing I-85, houses the most technologically advanced manufacturing, warehousing, packaging, and shipping operation in one highly efficient 220,000-square-foot facility.

The activities of the Spartanburg facility include a state-of-the-art nickel plating machine with an environmentally friendly water recycling system that far exceeds

government regulations. The newest addition to the plant is an A-frame computerized order-picking system that chooses and packs items with remarkable speed and accuracy.

As a natural extension of its slogan—Excellence Through Teamwork—Prym-Dritz strives to foster a family-like work atmosphere with open communication among its employees. Likewise, the employees have moved toward a structure based on high-performance work teams as part of the company's growing involvement in Total Quality Management. In fact, Prym-Dritz is the first company in its industry to adopt this progressive management philosophy, according to Dan Davis, vice president of sales and marketing.

"The biggest single factor in our success in Spartanburg has been attitude," says Mackey. "You can get things done here; there is a natural spirit of cooperation." And he believes it is that cooperative spirit—among the company's employees and throughout the community—that will ensure a successful future for Prym-Dritz.

Prym-Dritz manufactures and distributes a diversity of sewing notions and craft products, ranging from pins and needles to measuring tools and fabric dyes. The newest addition to the Spartanburg plant is an A-frame computerized order-picking system (above) that chooses and packs items with remarkable speed and accuracy.

The company's state-of-the-art nickel plating machine boasts an environmentally friendly water recycling system that far exceeds government regulations.

Flagstar Companies, Inc.

A SMALL FAST-FOOD RESTAURANT OPENED IN 1961 ON KENNEDY STREET IN DOWNTOWN Spartanburg and quickly became a favorite for teenagers, college students, and families. That restaurant—the first Hardee's franchise—still serves delicious "burgers and fries," as well as an expanded menu, while the company that started it has grown to be South Carolina's largest publicly held headquarters and the third largest food service company in the United States.

Flagstar Companies, Inc., known as TW Services until 1993, is a $3.7-billion firm employing approximately 120,000 people systemwide. Its two principal lines of business are restaurant chains through Denny's, Hardee's, Quincy's Family Steakhouse, and El Pollo Loco business units, and contract food, vending, and recreation services through Canteen Corporation.

Flagstar recently built a 17-story high-rise headquarters building on East Main Street in downtown Spartanburg.

Owned and operated by Flagstar since 1987, Denny's (top right) is the largest full-service family restaurant chain in the United States.

Also a part of the Flagstar family, Quincy's Family Steakhouse (bottom right) is a leading family restaurant chain in the Southeast.

POPULAR RESTAURANT CHAINS

Owned and operated by Flagstar since 1987, Denny's is the largest full-service family restaurant chain in the United States. With 1,500 units in 49 states and nine foreign countries, Denny's has come a long way from its beginnings in 1953 as a donut shop. Offering comfortable dining and moderately priced food, the chain is today well known for its Grand Slam™ menu and 24-hour service.

Flagstar, through a wholly owned subsidiary, also is the largest franchisee of Hardee's. The company currently operates over 550

restaurants located in nine South-eastern states, as well as Arkansas, Ohio, and Pennsylvania. In addition to hamburgers, fried chicken, hot dogs, and roast beef, fish, and chicken sandwiches, Hardee's offers a breakfast menu featuring its popular Made From Scratch™ biscuits, which account for approximately 39 percent of total annual sales.

Quincy's Family Steakhouse is a leading family restaurant chain in the Southeast. The first Quincy's opened in 1973 in nearby Greenville, serving steak entrees and related items. Flagstar acquired the chain in 1977 when it had only nine units in North and South Carolina. Less than two decades later, there are over 200 Quincy's restaurants in 10 states. In addition to a complete menu that includes the popular yeast roll, the chain offers a weekend breakfast bar and a daily buffet-style food bar called the "Country Sideboard."

Acquired by Flagstar in 1987, El Pollo Loco is the only major quick-service restaurant chain to specialize in flame-broiled chicken marinated in fruit juices, herbs, and spices. The chain recently introduced its first non-chicken offerings—steak fajitas, tacos, and burritos. Established in Mexico in 1975, El Pollo Loco entered the U.S. market in 1980 with a restaurant in Los Angeles. Today, there are over 200 El Pollo Loco units in California and Nevada. The chain is expanding into Japan, Guam, and the Philippines through licensing agreements.

FOOD SERVICE MANAGEMENT

Canteen Corporation is one of the largest contract food service management companies in the United States. Its two principal divisions—Food and Vending, and Recreation Services—operate in 48 states, Washington, D.C., and abroad.

The Food and Vending group provides on-site food service and vending at industrial plants, offices,

major financial institutions, and government installations, as well as hospitals, retirement centers, correctional facilities, and educational institutions. Canteen serves approximately 1,500 noncommercial food service accounts and 9,600 vending accounts.

The Recreation Services group provides concession services under contract to a number of state and national parks and special attractions. For example, Canteen serves five major baseball parks, including Yankee Stadium and Candlestick Park, and five professional football stadiums, including the Hubert H. Humphrey Metrodome, Los Ange-

Flagstar's goals are minority recruitment and training for management-level positions; greater franchise opportunities for minorities; a minority procurement program; and increased use of minority firms for professional services.

These goals have been incorporated into Flagstar's corporate mission to be the best food service company in the world by the year 2000. The company hopes to achieve this status through Mission 2000, a companywide service quality program.

"The people of Spartanburg have been very supportive of our company for more than 30 years," says Jerome J. Richardson, chairman and CEO of the company.

The first Hardee's franchise opened in 1961 on Kennedy Street in downtown Spartanburg. Today, Flagstar operates over 550 Hardee's restaurants located in nine Southeastern states, as well as Arkansas, Ohio, and Pennsylvania.

les Coliseum, and Tampa Stadium. The company also provides lodging, food services, and souvenirs to numerous federal government-contracted leisure operations, such as Yellowstone National Park, the Florida Everglades, Mount Rushmore National Park, the North Rim of the Grand Canyon, and the Kennedy Space Center.

AN IMPORTANT FORCE IN SPARTANBURG

Around Spartanburg, Flagstar is best known for its role in reviving the downtown area and diversifying the community's economic base.

In 1988 the company announced plans to build a 17-story high-rise headquarters building on East Main Street. Flagstar has since relocated many of its employees

and has moved the Chicago headquarters of Canteen Corporation and its Los Angeles-area Denny's offices to the downtown area. The company has also leased additional office space in the community to accommodate its 1,000-plus support staff. In the process, Flagstar has created a new spirit in Spartanburg—bringing people to the city's center and paving the way for a number of new retailers and businesses that are helping to further revitalize downtown.

A leader in its industry, Flagstar recently took a landmark step to provide greater opportunities for minorities. The comprehensive Fair Share Agreement signed with the NAACP will have an estimated value of over $1 billion in direct and indirect benefits from 1993 to the year 2000. Among

"We brought major divisions of Flagstar from Chicago and California here. This is an ideal place to teach the values we have lived by in our company over the years— hard work, teamwork and harmony, treating people fairly, and doing what you say you will do."

127

Sulzer Ruti Inc.

SULZER RUTI INC., A SUBSIDIARY OF THE SWISS-BASED FIRM SULZER RUTI LIMITED, WAS PART of a pioneer movement in the early 1960s when the company opened an office in Spartanburg to provide sales and service to its growing base of customers in the U.S. textile industry. At that time, there were very few international companies in the area, but Sulzer Ruti saw the potential for Spartanburg to become a hub of worldwide commerce and trade. Judging the situation today, the company is proud to have been a

trendsetter among international firms.

Sulzer Ruti is known worldwide for high-quality, reliable weaving machinery and today is the only company to offer machinery and replacement parts for all three insertion systems—rapier, projectile, and air-jet. The company prides itself on its after-sales service and credits its tremendous success over the years to this commitment to customer quality.

recipient of an engineering award from the internationally renowned Textile Institute for developments in weaving technology. Sulzer Ruti is constantly looking for new and better ways to serve the textile industry.

The company is also a community-minded citizen. In 1988, during its silver anniversary, Sulzer Ruti presented the Spartanburg Area Chamber of Commerce with a six-foot-tall globe made entirely of

company's employees can also be seen promoting Swiss culture during area festivals, such as the International Festival and Spring Fling.

Sulzer Ruti has grown and prospered along with Spartanburg in the past 30 years. The company started out with three employees and a 12,000-square-foot sales and service office. Today, it employs 75 people in a 60,000-square-foot facility offering technical and engineering services, training, installa-

Sulzer Ruti's 60,000-square-foot Spartanburg facility is located in the I-85 "boom belt" at Highway 9.

Textile World magazine, in its 1993 survey of the textile industry, ranked Sulzer Ruti first among all textile machinery suppliers.

Sulzer Ruti prides itself on the state-of-the-art technology available in its products. This technology is the result of heavy investment in research and development. The first ever successful shuttleless weaving machine—the projectile weaving machine—was introduced by Sulzer Ruti. This invention revolutionized the weaving industry. In 1982 the company was the

textile machinery parts to symbolize both Spartanburg's importance to the textile industry and the international growth rapidly taking place in the community. The company is involved in many area charities and is a proud participant in Textile Week activities.

In order to further enrich Spartanburg's international culture, Sulzer Ruti hosts an annual celebration of Swiss Independence Day on August 1 as part of its involvement with the Swiss American Society of the Piedmont. Many of the

tion, spare parts, and sales services. Sulzer Ruti looks forward to the future growth of both the company and the community.

Luciano Cont, president of Sulzer Ruti, emphasizes, "We are a highly technical company with the dedication to search new avenues and provide visionary technology to our customers. We have a deep commitment to our customers and to our community, and we feel both are equally committed to us."

Menzel, Inc.

T O CELEBRATE THE 25TH ANNIVERSARY OF THE ESTABLISHMENT OF MENZEL, INC. IN Spartanburg, President Gerd Menzel visited in 1990 from the company's headquarters in Bielefeld, West Germany. ◆ His mood was reflective as he reminisced about the first sales of Menzel machinery to textile companies in the early 1960s. He spoke of his friendship with Richard E. Tukey, who as executive vice president of the Spartanburg Area Chamber of Commerce helped establish Menzel in

Spartanburg—in just four days, including housing for the manager and articles of incorporation for the company. He recalled the day, years later, when he was made an honorary citizen of Spartanburg, and he reflected on the time Governor John West awarded him the Order of the Palmetto, the highest honor South Carolina's governor can bestow.

In 1992 his son, Hans-Joachim Menzel, provided another emotional moment as he spoke in front of Menzel's 80,000-square-foot Spartanburg facility facing I-85. Two 12-foot-tall slabs of the Berlin Wall were set into place as a gesture of good will to the United States and as thanks for the help America provided Germany after World War II.

These events, which symbolize the development of positive German-American relations in Spartanburg, were made possible by the success of Menzel, Inc. in the American marketplace.

GROWTH AND DIVERSIFICATION

Like most European companies coming to Spartanburg County in the 1960s and 1970s, Menzel began as a sales and service operation providing equipment to the South's emerging textile industry. The company soon realized it was more practical to build the equipment in Spartanburg, and in 1965 became the first European firm to manufacture textile machinery in South Carolina. "We used the basic design and technology of our German operation, and Americanized it," says General Manager Jochem Schoellkopf.

In 1964 Menzel introduced the first large-roll batching system to the U.S. textile industry. This innovative material handling system allows manufacturers to wind very large rolls of fabric onto fixed cores on portable carriages, resulting in time and cost savings. Known

in the industry as the A-frame system, this Menzel equipment is now used not only in textile manufacturing, but also in plastics, nonwovens, fiberglass, rubber, and other industrial applications. The company's 50 Spartanburg employees include a sophisticated engineering, sales, and service staff, as well as machinists and metalworkers.

Over the years, Menzel has developed a specialty in custom-designing machinery for splicing, chemical application, rewinding,

and winding. Using computer-aided design and computer numerically controlled manufacturing techniques, the company has developed expertise with many types of machinery. "Experience is our biggest asset," Schoellkopf says.

The Spartanburg operation has grown slowly and steadily to three times its original size and has diversified to produce some machinery not built by Menzel plants in Germany. In fact, less than 40 percent of Menzel's U.S. revenues today come from the textile industry. The company hopes to continue to expand its services into other markets to meet the needs of diverse manufacturers.

"We are determined to be constantly in touch with our customers, always responding to their needs," Schoellkopf says. "We are in a cooperative venture with our clients to make sure the relationship is beneficial to both our customers and our company."

Menzel's 80,000-square-foot Spartanburg facility facing I-85 has doubled and redoubled in size since 1965.

Menzel employs computer-aided design software to develop custom textile machinery for splicing, chemical application, rewinding, and winding (left).

Hoechst Celanese Corporation

Hoechst Celanese Corporation's Spartanburg plant is a broadly diversified, constantly modernizing, community-involved manufacturer of polyester products that touch many aspects of modern life. ◆ The roots of the 1,600-employee operation are deep in sophisticated chemistry and the development of creative uses of polyester—the world's most readily recyclable material—for end-use applications by customers throughout North America and other parts of the world. The Spartanburg plant includes more than 2 million square feet of operations floor space on a 670-acre site.

Hoechst Celanese and its German parent, Hoechst AG, are the world's leading producers of polyester fibers and yarns.

DIVERSIFICATION

The Spartanburg plant is the company's major producer of polyester staple: short lengths of fiber for both textile and industrial/technical applications.

Trevira® polyester staple produced at the Spartanburg plant is utilized in the apparel, floor cover-

The Spartanburg plant includes more than 2 million square feet of operations floor space on a 670-acre site (above right).

The Cigarette Bullet is manufactured from Trevira® polyester spunbond fabrics for performance and aesthetics (right).

ings, and home furnishings markets. In addition, Spartanburg employees manufacture Trevira® polyester spunbond and Trevira® polyester monofilament products, as well as polyester polymer resins.

Polyester spunbond is principally used in roofing and geotextile end applications. Geotextiles are important in a wide variety of civil engineering end uses. For example, these fabrics are used as filter media or separators in subsurface drainage systems, in the stabilization of embankments and the containment of silt runoff from erodible slopes, in the construction of landfills, and in the construction of access roads, railroads, and parking and storage areas over soft, unstable soil.

Polyester monofilament products from the Spartanburg plant are used in zippers, in conveyor belting, and in dryer and forming-screen applications in the paper industry. Polyester polymer resins

produced at the Spartanburg plant are used extensively in the manufacture of soft drink bottles, food packaging, and pharmaceutical and other custom containers, as well as in the manufacture of polyester fibers at other locations.

MODERNIZATION

Hoechst Celanese has in recent years invested nearly $200 million toward modernizing overall Spartanburg plant operations to enhance the cost-competitiveness of its products in the global marketplace.

The Spartanburg plant has recently completed the installation and start-up of nearly 100 million annual pounds of high-technology staple-fiber production capacity. Additional major investments have been made to upgrade and expand monofilament, spunbond, and resins capacity to state-of-the-art standards. The Spartanburg operation also figures prominently in the company's plans for adding more than 500 million pounds of polyester resins capacity in North America by 1995.

These projects will allow Hoechst Celanese to further strengthen its packaging resins focus on the clear soft drink bottle and custom-container segments of the packaging market, as it selectively cultivates higher value-added opportunities for food tray, thermo-forming, and extrusion-blow-molded applications.

RESPONSIBLE CITIZENSHIP

"The words 'because we care,'" says Spartanburg plant Site Manager Bill Mayrose, "aptly summarize why the employees and management of this facility are so active in and contribute so significantly to community-enrichment activities."

A prime example of that caring is the more than 440 pints of blood donated by Hoechst Celanese employees each year during Red Cross Bloodmobile visits to the plant. Another is the giving record of Spartanburg plant employees, who have from 1990 through 1993 given or pledged $615,568 to the United Way.

That caliber of responsible citizenship is rooted in large measure in the multifaceted statement of spirit and vision developed and implemented by Spartanburg plant personnel. It proclaims, in part: "We take pride in who we are and what we do and are recognized individually and in teams for our achievements. We shape our future such that job fulfillment, high self-esteem, and acceptance of diversity are a way of life. We are enthusiastic, secure, respected and informed . . . .The Spartanburg plant is recognized as a great place to work."

CARING FOR THE ENVIRONMENT

Another portion of the employee vision statement addresses the close relationship between proper care of the environment and plant operations. Consequently, there is

consistent, serious attention to meeting or exceeding government and industry environmental standards.

Examples of environmental initiatives being implemented include emission-reduction efforts and solid waste reduction. Through recycling, reuse, and source reduction, solid waste from Spartanburg plant operations disposed of in landfills has decreased by approxi-

mately 55 percent since 1989. Further reduction opportunities have been identified and are in progress. Overall, through 1992, the Spartanburg plant's chemical emissions have been reduced 30 percent from 1988 levels and will reach 50 percent for the year 1993. The downward trend will continue through at least 1996.

To ensure continual improvement in environmental efforts, the plant initiated a Community Advi-

sory Panel. The group, which includes 12 neighbors and members of the local community, advises plant staff on environmental matters and provides a means of communication with the local community.

"We are keenly aware," says Mayrose, "of our many roles as an international manufacturer, as a major employer, and as a corporate resident and neighbor within our community."

COMMUNITY INVOLVEMENT

Hoechst Celanese is especially proud of its contributions to and participation in community involvement efforts in Spartanburg and Upstate South Carolina. Through the Spartanburg plant, the company contributes more than $100,000 annually to help finance local education, health and human services, cultural, civic, and public affairs organizations and activities. Among the many benefactors are Converse, Wofford, Spartanburg Methodist, and Spartanburg Technical colleges; the Spartanburg Arts Council and Little Theater; the Boys' and Girls' Club of Metro Spartanburg; Junior Achievement; and AWARE Literacy Council.

Spartanburg plant employees also give generously of their personal time and talents in a variety of ways, many of them connected with improving educational opportunities in the city and county. Such employee/company involvement in 1992 and 1993 won three awards of excellence from the South Carolina Department of Education.

Mayrose explains, "Young people are the employees and the consumers of the future. We are pleased to help in any way possible in the development of their full potential to become effective leaders of tomorrow."

From top to bottom at left:
This spinnerette is the starting point where molten polymer is converted into fiber.

Monofilaments are wound on spools for shipment to Hoechst Celanese customers, who weave them into huge industrial fabrics.

A control room operator monitors the computerized polymerization process.

Zimmer Machinery America

THE ZIMMER FAMILY HAS BEEN INVOLVED IN THE TEXTILE INDUSTRY SINCE 1874, WHEN Franz Zimmer started his own company in the town of Varnsdorf in what is today the Czech Republic. The Zimmer Company, now based in Klagenfurt and Kufstein, Austria, is a world leader in producing printing equipment and auxiliary machinery for the textile industry. ◆ The company's only manufacturing facility outside Austria is located in northeast Spartanburg County near Cowpens. Zimmer has worldwide sales offices and its own sales and service facilities in many locations, such as Hong Kong, Shanghai, the United Kingdom, Mexico, and Argentina.

"It is our commitment to provide a complete line of machines to our specific market," says President Roland J.P. Zimmer (right), adding that the company works closely with its customers to develop equipment that meets their needs.

MORE THAN A CENTURY OF GROWTH

One of the first products Zimmer produced was a can dryer for textiles. Later the company began manufacturing roller gravure printing machines for textiles, and the operation was expanded to include a foundry employing several hundred workers.

Following World War II, the Zimmer family moved the company to Austria. Today, under the management of Johannes Zimmer Sr. and his family, the company maintains four factories in Klagenfurt and Kufstein. Employing about 750 people, these operations develop and manufacture textile printing equipment, including rotary and flat screen printing machines with magnetically con-

trolled roller squeegees, and other printing machines for the carpet and textile industries. The research and development center near the main office in Klagenfurt has developed a series of revolutionary processes, and the company holds more than 100 patents worldwide.

In 1969 Zimmer Machinery established a small sales office in Spartanburg County to offer sales, start-up, and service of Zimmer equipment. That operation has continued to grow and expand over the years, adding office, warehouse, and then manufacturing space. In 1985 Zimmer Machinery Corporation was incorporated in the United States. A new manufacturing facility, completed in October 1992 at the Spartanburg County offices, doubled the size of the operation to 40,000 square feet. About 50 people are employed at the facility, which in addition to conducting marketing, sales, and service activities, manufactures parts for Zimmer machines.

ADVANCED TECHNOLOGY AND SERVICE

Zimmer is one of only a few companies in the world to manufacture the type of equipment it produces. According to Rudi Doujak, executive vice president and CEO of the Spartanburg County facility, the company takes that responsibility very seriously. Zimmer places great emphasis on research and development to apply the latest technology, to improve quality, and to increase the productivity of its equipment.

"The machines are very precise because once the fabric is printed, which happens in a split second, mistakes cannot be corrected," says President Roland J.P. Zimmer. The newest generation of Zimmer's machinery is fully computerized so that 100 percent pattern repeatability is guaranteed.

"It is our commitment to provide a complete line of machines to our specific market," he says, adding that the company works closely with its customers to develop equipment that meets their needs. "Zimmer Machinery provides one-stop solutions for our customers. Our staff can discuss any printing and finishing need with them and work towards finding the best solution."

Adds Doujak, "One of our greatest assets is that we develop true partnerships with our customers. A foundation of trust and friendship is important in every one of our business transactions."

A new manufacturing facility, completed in October 1992, brought Zimmer's Spartanburg County operation to 40,000 square feet.

General Travel, Inc.

TWENTY-FOUR-YEAR-OLD GENERAL TRAVEL IS BECOMING THE TRAVEL MANAGEMENT company of choice in the Spartanburg area thanks to new ownership, improved location, and an emphasis on outstanding service. ◆ "Travel companies face a true challenge because they cannot compete on the basis of price," says Hunter Huss, president and CEO. "Airline ticket pricing and travel agency commissions are the same for everyone because they are set by the airline industry. Where

General shines is in service." Huss adds that the company accomplishes this through the quality of its staff and by keeping abreast of the latest technology.

General has one of the highest staff-to-client ratios in the travel industry. Likewise, its agents average more than 11 years in the business, and none has less than eight years of experience. The company's agents are supported by highly qualified staff.

General Travel uses the most thorough computerized information management system of any travel company in the Upstate, allowing it to provide comprehensive travel planning, detailed data analysis of client expenditures, and even satellite ticket printing at the client's office. The system continually checks published prices and automatically enters client information when the lowest fares or most convenient flight times become available. These services, among others, have made General the agency of choice among many business travelers and corporate clients.

NEW OWNERSHIP BRINGS POSITIVE CHANGE

General Travel began in 1969 as a full-service travel agency. In 1991 it was purchased by Hunter Huss, a former stockbroker, and two partners, who brought about a major management change. In addition to relocating the business to Converse Corners Center near the intersection of St. John and East Main streets, the new owners expanded company services, placing a greater emphasis on executive and business

travel management. Later that year, General's purchase of another area travel agency strengthened its expertise in leisure travel.

Among the company's corporate clients are many international

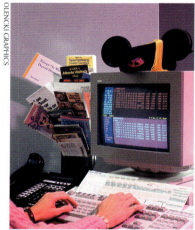

companies. "Our international clients are the backbone of the company," says Huss. "And our relationships with carriers and services at points of destination abroad are excellent."

According to Huss, General has no standard corporate contract and no standard proposal for one.

"If a prospective client wants to talk about corporate travel, we bring nothing to the meeting but a legal pad and a couple of questions: What do you need? What do you expect?" says Huss. The answers

may range from managing travel budgets more carefully to consolidating expense accounting or implementing new travel policies.

"No two clients are the same," he adds. "Meeting the client's needs and expectations is a process. We come first to listen, and we keep listening throughout our relationship."

General has seen dramatic growth in its second year of new ownership. And Huss says the company is positioned for continued growth. He envisions additional locations in the future but stresses that customer satisfaction is General's primary objective: "Our goal is not to be the biggest travel agency, but the best. Offering the most responsive, thorough, and professional travel service is the most important aspect of our business."

"Meeting the client's needs and expectations is a process. We come first to listen, and we keep listening throughout our relationship," says Hunter Huss, president and CEO.

General Travel uses the most thorough computerized information management system of any travel company in the Upstate, allowing it to provide comprehensive travel planning, detailed data analysis of client expenditures, and even satellite ticket printing at the client's office.

Zima Corporation, Kusters Corporation, and EVAC Corporation

ACCORDING TO GEORGE BERNARD SHAW, "THE PEOPLE WHO GET ON IN THIS WORLD are the people who get up and look for the circumstances they want, and if they can't find them, make them." Kurt Zimmerli, chairman of Zima Corporation, Kusters Corporation, and EVAC Corporation, has done both. ◆ More than 20 years ago, Swiss-born Zimmerli found Spartanburg to be an ideal location to start Zima Corporation. "Eighty percent of the textile industry lay within a 300-mile radius of

Spartanburg, and the city offered an excellent business climate," he says. Zimmerli then created less tangible, but no less important, circumstances for the company to succeed: a clear mission for the operation and a strong emphasis on customer relationships. Zima began doing business in 1969.

The same conditions supported Zima's efforts when it

chinery companies. In essence, Zima acts as a general contractor for its clients. A customer describes its needs for a manufacturing operation, then Zima helps determine the best combination of equipment to fulfill those needs. Zima performs all necessary functions to purchase and install equipment and then trains operators for best performance of the equipment.

EVAC specializes in the application of vacuum technology to textile processes. Vacuum systems reduce energy usage, protect the environment, and enhance the customer's ability to control equipment processes. One major application of vacuum systems is controlling the application and removal of liquids and chemicals from fabric during finishing. EVAC equipment

Zima, Kusters, and EVAC are headquartered together on a handsomely landscaped campus facing I-85.

joined Eduard Kusters to establish Kusters Corporation in 1974 and when Kusters Corporation acquired EVAC Corporation of Spartanburg in 1991. "Our vision is to be the best suppliers to the textile industry in our fields. We specialize and keep our focus on what we know best," Zimmerli says.

Zima and Kusters are located next to one another on a handsomely landscaped campus facing I-85. EVAC is located in the Kusters facility and is operating worldwide.

THREE DIVERSE PURPOSES

Although linked by ownership, the three companies are diverse in their expertise.

Zima Corporation is an engineering-oriented marketing firm, representing Kusters, EVAC, and a number of European textile ma-

Kusters Corporation manufactures textile dyeing and finishing equipment, with significant success in the carpet industry. A joint venture of Zima and Eduard Kusters Maschinenfabrik of Krefeld, Germany, Kusters is recognized as the leader in its field. Today, 90 percent of all carpets dyed in the United States are processed on Kusters equipment. The company also exports its machinery.

"To have built, then maintained our market share over 20 years is a remarkable achievement for us," says Blas Miyares, president of Kusters. "It is due to our outstanding associates and Kusters' commitment to continuous research and development. Our emphasis on staying at the forefront of technology has helped the U.S. carpet industry remain current and successful."

is sold as part of a new installation, as an improvement to existing equipment, and in stand-alone applications.

All three companies are dedicated to total quality, emphasizing customer service and continuous quality improvement. Their 120 associates, who include professional engineers, textile technicians, and textile technologists, are committed to making the quality program a success.

"We have been successful over a long period of time because of the integrity, dedication, and effort of our associates, many of whom have been with us from the beginning," says Zimmerli. "Our people are the key to our excellent relationships with our suppliers and customers—and to the continued success of Zima, Kusters, and EVAC."

The Prudential Reed & Young Realty

BROADENING ITS EXPERTISE AS SPARTANBURG COUNTY'S NUMBER ONE REAL ESTATE FIRM IN listings and sales, The Prudential Reed & Young Realty has developed strong capabilities in relocation services for corporations and families moving into the Spartanburg area. ◆ "Our goal is to minimize stress and maximize results for all parties involved in a relocation process," says Evelyn Young, broker and vice president, who with Cullen Reed founded the company in 1976. With a 50-agent staff, Prudential

Reed & Young has offices at 114 Southport Road, 951 East Main Street, and 2795 Reidville Road. The company is associated with The Prudential Real Estate Affiliates, Inc., a subsidiary of The Prudential, America's largest insurance company.

In addition to its real estate and relocation services, Prudential Reed & Young includes Cullen Reed Construction Company, a third-generation firm that has been building custom homes in the Spartanburg area since 1950.

RELOCATION EXPERTS

Several key affiliations make Prudential Reed & Young an outstanding choice for businesses and families seeking relocation services.

The company is a member of Prudential Relocation Affiliates, the arm of The Prudential real estate subsidiary that specializes in assisting corporations involved in moving groups of transferees. "Through The Prudential, we have status as a nationally recognized relocation service and access to other highly professional and experienced personnel in the network," says Young.

In addition, since 1992 Reed & Young has been a member and part owner of The Prudential Carolinas Realty, an organization composed of a number of real estate firms throughout North and South Carolina that are members of Prudential Real Estate Affiliates, Inc. It is the largest real estate company serving both North and South Carolina. With 34 offices in seven major regional markets, The Prudential Carolinas Realty offers the strongest relocation team in the Carolinas, composed of 20 full-time relocation specialists who have access to an international referral network of more than 1,900 offices worldwide.

Finally, the firm is a member of Relocation Specialists, an asso-

ciation of six local real estate firms that offer a full range of corporate transferee services for the Greenville-Spartanburg area. The association offers a single point of contact and a comprehensive follow-through for corporations moving into the Spartanburg area.

H. Cullen Reed Jr., vice president, and Evelyn K. Young, CRB, vice president, founded the company in 1976.

Relocation Specialists coordinates all details of a move in a smooth and informative manner and serves as a liaison between the corporation and the community—ensuring a positive transition and enabling employees to become productive as quickly as possible. Services include temporary housing assistance, area tours, family orientation services, and rental assistance.

The Prudential Reed & Young Realty is a hometown company dedicated to its community. Reed and Young, both lifelong residents of Spartanburg County, are active in many professional and civic endeavors that help improve the quality of life in the area. Along with their company employees, they are dedicated to being "a family of friends" to the community—its newcomers included.

The Prudential Reed & Young Realty is committed to making every move a happy one (far left).

Debra Giles (left), relocation director, spearheads the firm's relocation services for corporations and families moving into the Spartanburg area.

Staubli Corporation

THE STAUBLI GROUP—HEADQUARTERED IN SWITZERLAND AND THE PARENT COMPANY of Staubli Corporation in Spartanburg County—is the world's largest manufacturer of a complete range of highly specialized shed formation machines used on all types of weaving machines. The company has also found recent success in the manufacture and distribution of hydraulic and pneumatic couplings, where Staubli sees its largest market potential.

In 1988 Staubli moved into a newly constructed 30,000-square-foot building in Duncan in the airport area.

Staubli Corporation, today employing 62 people, offers sales and service of shedding machinery and hydraulic and pneumatic products for customers in the United States, Canada, and Mexico.

Founded in Horgen, Switzerland, in 1892, the Staubli Group serves industries worldwide from manufacturing facilities in Switzerland, France, Germany, Italy, Great Britain, Brazil, and Japan. The U.S. sales, service, and distribution office is located at the Hillside Park of Commerce near Interstate 85 in Duncan, South Carolina.

"Shedding machinery is the brain of the loom, telling it what design to weave into the fabric," explains Harald Behrend, vice president and general manager of Staubli Corporation. It is estimated that the Staubli Group, through its corporate headquarters and subsidiaries, provides shedding machinery for 85 percent of the looms sold worldwide. The Duncan facility alone has been successful in supplying approximately 65 percent of the Jacquard shedding machines sold in the North American market. These machines are the most sophisticated shedding machines being made worldwide.

The Staubli companies also manufacture hydraulic and pneumatic couplings and multicoupling systems for the steel, plastics, automotive, and aviation industries.

"These products are needed for all types of equipment in multiple industries," says Behrend, noting that it has been a successful diversification.

The company recently signed a global cooperation contract with Cincinnati Milacron, a leading manufacturer of injection molding equipment. In addition, Staubli entered the robotics field through the 1988 purchase of Unimation, Inc., a division of Westinghouse.

A U.S. PRESENCE SINCE 1953

Staubli entered the U.S. market in 1953, represented by H.J. Theiler Corp., which had operations in Whitinsville, Massachusetts, and Spartanburg, South Carolina. "Our products were so successful that in 1979 we had to set up our own U.S. organization," says Behrend.

Staubli Corporation, today employing 62 people, offers sales and service of shedding machinery and hydraulic and pneumatic products for customers in the United States, Canada, and Mexico. It also has just begun limited manufacturing of hydraulic and pneumatic coupling products.

Over the years, the company has moved to several different facilities to accommodate growth. In 1988 Staubli Corporation moved into a newly constructed 30,000-square-foot building in Duncan in the airport area. "Proximity to the airport is vital," says Behrend, "because Staubli engineers and technicians visit customers nationwide, and the Duncan facility receives many overseas visitors." The company plans to add 10,000 to 12,000 square feet of office space in the near future.

Staubli Corporation is a very active member of the community through its involvement with the University of South Carolina at Spartanburg. "Staubli is committed to furthering international business education by helping young people develop the skills necessary for the world market," says Behrend. "Every year we place several students from the Master of Business Administration program in internships with our European affiliates."

In all its activities, Staubli Corporation strives for the high standards set by its parent company, which has been family-owned since its founding at the turn of the century. "We have found success," says Behrend, "by operating under Staubli's longtime motto of quality, high performance, and leadership in technological advances."

Saxonia-Franke of America, Inc.

WHEN A CYCLIST PULLS ON STRETCH SHORTS FOR A RIDE, SAXONIA-FRANKE OF America probably produced parts for the machine that made the shorts. When a driver buckles a seat belt, the click may indicate that a Saxonia-Franke part has slid into position. In applications as diverse as these in literally hundreds of end uses, Saxonia-Franke supplies precision parts and, more recently, assembled component parts to a growing base of customers worldwide.

Saxonia-Franke GmbH was established in Goeppingen in the Federal Republic of Germany by Hilmar Franke in 1947. The company soon became a major producer of flat stamped parts for knitting machines and hosiery machines. Saxonia-Franke was one of the first metal stampers to adopt fineblanking, a special stamping process developed in Europe in the 1950s. In growing demand today, fineblanking improves repeatability and accuracy as well as the quality of the stamped part.

Over the years Saxonia-Franke has systematically diversified the applications of its processes. Today, its parts are used not only in textile machinery, but also in automobiles, business machines, computers, and household appliances, among many other products.

OLENCKI GRAPHICS

SPARTANBURG PLANT OPENED IN 1979

The company established a U.S. plant, Saxonia-Franke of America, in Spartanburg in 1979. Staffed with three employees, the plant began producing precision stamped parts for warp knitting machinery. In 1985, armed with new equipment and expanded manufacturing capabilities, the company received its first order for fineblanked parts. Consistent growth ensued, and the company today employs 60 workers in Spartanburg.

In 1992 Hilmar Franke's son, Michael, purchased Saxonia-Franke of America and all its operations. "Our sales have increased dramatically as we have expanded awareness of the applications of our processes," says Michael Franke, who lives in Spartanburg and serves

as company president. "We foresee doubling, perhaps tripling, the size of our operation in Spartanburg over the next five years."

Fineblanking is expected to continue to be a growing market as craftsmen become more skilled in its applications and as manufacturers demand more precision and accuracy in parts. "One of our specialties is helping customers discover ways they can design their processes and machinery to include fineblanked parts," says Gary Watchorn, general manager for the Fineblanking Division of Saxonia-Franke.

Another area of growth is expected to come from the company's new subsidiary, Component Sales, which was formed in Spartanburg in mid-1993. Component Sales

offers its customers the wide array of processes of the Saxonia-Franke operation but expands those capabilities by offering the complete assembly or subassembly of components that may include high-speed stampings, multislide stampings, laser processes, screw machine processes, photo etching, and precision molded plastics. This will give customers the benefit of having a single-source supplier for a wide variety of parts.

"Our people have the know-how and the ability not only to meet the demands of the marketplace but to anticipate them," says Michael Franke of the dynamic company that is proud to call Spartanburg home.

Since the company's U.S. plant was established in Spartanburg in 1979, Saxonia-Franke of America has undergone significant growth.

Cleveland-White Realtors

"**W**HEN PEOPLE ASK ME WHAT WE SPECIALIZE IN, I TELL THEM REAL ESTATE." Arthur Cleveland of Cleveland-White Realtors says this with tongue in cheek, but his statement rings true. In a time of intense specialization and niche marketing, Cleveland-White has risen to powerhouse status in the Spartanburg real estate industry by approaching almost any project as "doable." ◆ Cleveland-White is the Spartanburg area's only truly diversified real estate company. Since

1982 when the firm was founded, its name has been synonymous with high-quality residential, commercial, and industrial sales and development in Spartanburg County and throughout South Carolina and Georgia. "Excellence in everything we do is our goal," says Cleveland.

The firm is among the area's top five in residential real estate, with one-fourth of its 20 agents earning a place in the prestigious Million-Dollar Club. Adhering to the motto, "Our people—that's the difference," Cleveland says he favors having the best Realtors in the community rather than the most Realtors of any firm.

"Whether we're selling a home or working on a major commercial or residential development project, we insist that the quality match this community's highest expectations," says Arthur Cleveland, president.

The firm recently completed Converse Corners (top right), a charming mini-center containing retail stores, offices, and a restaurant.

Cleveland-White is also a leader in commercial sales and leasing, full-service property management, and full-service residential, commercial, office, and industrial development. The company recently joined a six-firm Greenville-Spartanburg consortium called Relocation Specialists and employs a full-time relocation director to help companies move their employees to the region.

COMMUNITY SUCCESS STORIES

Cleveland-White was an early developer of Spartanburg's now-booming West Side. Beginning with a commercial center along W.O. Ezell Boulevard, the company has been responsible for some of that area's outstanding projects, including Market Square. It has also been successful with Broadwalk, an office and retail development in downtown Spartanburg at Converse and Broad streets.

More recently, the firm completed Converse Corners, a charming mini-center containing retail stores, offices, and a restaurant, which adjoins Cleveland-White's home office on East Main Street across from Converse College.

"We don't look just to the large projects, though," says Cleveland. "We're just as pleased with the success of smaller projects, such as Maurice's barbecue restaurant and the Putt-Putt miniature golf course, which has already undergone three expansions." During its decade in business, Cleveland-White has produced office buildings as small as 4,000 square feet for a single tenant, up to the 66,000-square-foot multi-tenant Doctor's Medical Center near Spartanburg Regional Medical Center.

The firm also is known for its ability to move a project and get things done. For example, retail and office tenants moved into

Converse Corners just four months after construction began.

The firm is a "mover and shaker" in volunteer efforts throughout the community, as well. Attend a hearing on signage ordinances or land use, and Cleveland-White will be there. Look at the rosters of participants in Chamber of Commerce programs for improving community services or local schools, and Cleveland-White will be represented. Most agents and staff of the firm are involved in

programs that improve the quality of life in the Spartanburg area, such as schools for the handicapped, arts organizations, and city beautification or low-income housing improvement efforts.

RIVER FALLS PLANTATION

Local growth over the past decade has brought an abundance of recreational, cultural, and shopping amenities to both Spartanburg and Greenville, which anchor the ends of a 17-mile manufacturing region along Interstate 85. One of Cleveland-White's most exciting new projects, River Falls Plantation, is meeting an important need in this booming area.

"River Falls Plantation came to be because there was no high-quality residential area that could serve both communities," says Cleveland. "There also was not a residential community with a fee-only golf course, and we determined that could be a great boon for the area."

For the River Falls golf course, Cleveland-White and partner Gramling Brothers Realtors engaged the services of legendary golf pro Gary Player. "We asked him to design a course the public would both enjoy and find challenging and to put his signature on it," says Cleveland. The result is an 18-hole, par 72 golf course—one

of the Upstate's most exciting. Opened in 1990 with four sets of tees, the course offers an interesting mix of shots to test the imagination and skills of golfers of all ability levels.

Most of the 300 River Falls Plantation homesites, more than half of which have already been sold, overlook the golf course. With homes 2,000 square feet or more on 3/4-acre sites, the development also features lakes, streams, the South Tyger River, and lush vegetation to create a resort-like atmosphere. A clubhouse with swimming pool provides further opportunities for recreation and relaxation.

The 470-acre River Falls Plantation is located just off Interstate 85 near the intersection of Highway 290 and Reidville Road— eight miles from the Greenville-Spartanburg Airport, 15 miles from downtown Greenville, and 11 miles from downtown Spartanburg. This prime location provides residents easy access to theaters, museums, the Upstate's finest medical facilities, shopping malls, and the area's seven colleges and universities.

Says Cleveland, "Whether we're selling a home or working on a major commercial or residential development project, we insist that the quality match this community's highest expectations."

River Falls Plantation, a 470-acre development located just off Interstate 85 near the intersection of Highway 290 and Reidville Road, includes 300 homesites and an 18-hole, par 72 golf course.

SEW-Eurodrive, Inc.

SEW-Eurodrive, Inc. has built a reputation worldwide as a reliable provider of high-quality power transmissions. Its manufacturing and assembly facilities in Lyman, just west of Spartanburg, house the company's U.S. headquarters and handle the sales and assembly function for the Southeast region of the United States. The 200,000-square-foot plant also supplies gear components for assembly centers in 26 countries, making it one of the largest exporters in Spartanburg County. Approximately 75 percent of the product manufactured by SEW-Eurodrive in Lyman is exported.

SEW-Eurodrive's assembly center in Lyman, South Carolina, builds and supplies helical bevel gear units capable of up to 460 hp for customers throughout North America.

The Best in Employees and Equipment

Established in Bruchsal, Germany, in 1931, SEW-Eurodrive is today one of the world's largest gear producers, with 6,000 employees and annual sales of about $700 million. Eurodrive gearmotors and speed reducers are used in virtually every industry—from food and beverage processing to ski lifts and amusement rides, to industrial material-handling and lumber-process equipment, to water pollution control and waste-to-energy equipment.

Gear technology is over 2,000 years old, and continued growth is dependent on meeting the requirements of a highly technical and rapidly changing market. SEW-Eurodrive has made a commitment to continue developing and marketing the electronic drives and systems components necessary to maintain its position of leadership in the gear industry.

An equal commitment has been made to provide products of the highest possible quality. The company's major production plants in Germany are ISO 9001 certified, and steps for ISO 9002 qualification are under way in the United States and at all other facilities.

Committed to Spartanburg County

SEW-Eurodrive decided to open its Spartanburg County facility in 1983 for many of the same reasons other European corporations have come to the area. The company was attracted by the good transportation system, available land, an excellent work force, and the helpfulness of the local and state governments.

Over the years, SEW-Eurodrive's success in Lyman has been driven by the expertise and dedication of the 160 local employees who manufacture and assemble its products. Using the latest in numerical control and computerized numerical control machinery, the plant prides itself on its quality product and labor productivity.

No single customer accounts for more than 2 percent of SEW-Eurodrive's business in the United States, and the uses of its products are unusually diverse. These factors have helped buffer the company from economic swings, and growth has exceeded initial expectations.

Striving to be more than a good employer, SEW-Eurodrive has become actively involved in the area's educational community. For example, teachers from local schools work in the manufacturing and assembly areas setting up employee training programs during the summer months. SEW-Eurodrive employees help the schools understand how math is used in industry, and teachers help the company learn how to teach and train.

SEW-Eurodrive is also involved in the Business-Education Partnerships program of the Spartanburg Area Chamber of Commerce and the Tech Scholars program at Spartanburg Technical College. Through the latter initiative, local students can gain valuable work experience while earning an associate degree in a technological field.

For a decade now, quality products, efficient manufacturing processes, outstanding employees, and a commitment to the community in which it does business have led to unqualified success for SEW-Eurodrive in Spartanburg County.

One Price Clothing Stores, Inc.

ONE PRICE CLOTHING WAS STARTED IN 1984 WITH THE CONCEPT OF OFFERING THE best value available for one low price every day. Now, One Price Clothing Stores, Inc. is one of America's fastest growing women's apparel chains, with over 500 stores in 24 states. ◆ Henry D. Jacobs Jr., a third-generation retailer, had developed a keen knowledge of retailing. In 1914 his grandfather bought The Standard, a downtown Spartanburg clothing store. His stepfather later purchased the

business and ran it until 1969. Jacobs stepped in at that time and began expanding the company, opening Jakes, The Standard, and Gals Direct To You stores in Columbia, Greenville, Gaffney, Anderson, and Myrtle Beach. Jacobs sold his interest in the business to his sons shortly after the start of One Price Clothing.

Jacobs, along with Raymond Waters, a well-known Spartanburg CPA, opened the first store on August 23, 1984, in the Waccamaw Pottery Outlet (now Foothills Factory Stores). It was an immediate success. Customers welcomed the idea of an honest, everyday low price. Unlike other off-price retailers, the Spartanburg company offered a neat, easy-to-shop store with good service and a liberal return policy. Operating out of the store's back room, Jacobs and Waters did it all, from buying merchandise to finding locations for more stores. The second store, another success, opened in Gaffney on October 5. When the third store opened on November 21 in Greenville, they knew their unique concept was a hit.

The company's initial selling price was $6 for apparel, with accessories priced in multiples of $6. That price was maintained for six years until operating costs forced an increase of $1. The company fulfills its customers' needs by offering in-season fashion apparel and accessories for misses, juniors, women's plus sizes, and children. It purchases only first-quality merchandise. One Price Clothing's buyers take advantage of manufacturers' overproduction and other retailers' cancellations of orders.

This opportunistic method of buying allows One Price Clothing to sell every item at substantial discounts for a single price, now $7.

Rapid growth has been a driving force behind change for One Price Clothing. When operating

out of the back room of the first store became inadequate, Jacobs and Waters purchased property on Highway 290 in Duncan to build a corporate headquarters and distribution center. As the company has grown, it has expanded its corporate facilities three times. The building, now 390,000 square feet, sits on an 80-acre site and can accommodate expansion up to 800 stores.

Much of the company's success can be attributed to the individuals who run it on a daily basis. More and more people have joined One Price Clothing to perform crucial operations such as buying, allocating, distributing, and selling merchandise. More than 3,500 associates are now employed in the headquarters/distribution center and in the stores.

The original spirit of entrepreneurship is still evident throughout One Price Clothing today. Its associates thrive on the challenge of maintaining the One Price vision while successfully expanding the company to a nationwide chain of 1,000 stores by 1998.

One Price Clothing Stores is one of America's fastest growing women's apparel chains, with over 500 stores in 24 states.

Unlike other off-price retailers, One Price offers a neat, easy-to-shop store with good service and a liberal return policy.

The company's 390,000-square-foot headquarters in Duncan sits on an 80-acre site and can accommodate expansion up to 800 stores.

Residence Inn by Marriott

A HOTEL CAN NEVER BE QUITE LIKE HOME, BUT RESIDENCE INN, WITH ITS EXCEPTIONAL extended-stay amenities, comes closer than most. Residence Inn by Marriott is specifically designed to bring comfort and a lot of special attention to people who must stay away from home for more than a few days. ◆ "Our guests become family while they are with us," says Nancy Lee, manager of Spartanburg's 88-unit Residence Inn, located just six miles from the Greenville-Spartanburg Airport at

the intersection of Interstates 85 and 26. "Our goal is to exceed their expectations every day, every stay."

The dedicated staff members at Residence Inn Spartanburg enjoy the challenge of going beyond the call of duty for their guests, who may be transferring from another city or another country, in town on a demanding assignment, or undergoing an intensive training program. Residence Inn also hosts families that, because of a job transfer, are looking for new homes or checking out schools. The average stay is two weeks, but can run much longer.

Residence Inn by Marriott is committed to making guest stays as close to home as possible.

FIRST IMPRESSIONS

Guests know as soon as they enter the property, which has won several landscaping awards, that they are in for a special stay. Check-in takes place at the spacious and attractive Gatehouse building, where guests often play chess or browse in the library under its cathedral ceiling. Later, at hospitality hour,

Gatehouse activity steps up as tables are spread with complimentary food and beverages, and guests unwind and make new friends. In the summer, there are frequent cookouts with free hamburgers and hot dogs and, for the energetic, volleyball games. Every morning the Gatehouse offers beverages, fresh fruit, cereals, bagels, muffins, and hot breakfast items such as pancakes or sausage biscuits.

Each guest has a private, secured entrance to his or her unit, all of which are suites designed for either two or four guests. Each suite includes a fully equipped kitchen, a living area, and a separate dressing room and bath. Units designed for four have two sleeping areas on two stories for privacy, two bathrooms, and two television sets. Many units have fireplaces, with logs available at the Gatehouse.

A first-night guest will find the room's light on and soft music playing. The TV will be set to CNN for

the business traveler who may have missed the day's news. A First Nighter Kit in the kitchen includes coffee, tea, and microwave popcorn. International travelers are often greeted with a welcome basket that includes area information and a selection of ethnic foods. A note on the refrigerator from Lee says "Welcome Home" and gives instructions for contacting her.

And she truly wants to hear from every resident, to help with whatever is needed—grocery shopping, for instance, which is a free service. Lee and her staff also are happy to run other errands or make special arrangements, such as organizing a tour of schools, making reservations for golf, or picking up a video for the kids.

Special touches are another bonus at the Residence Inn. For example, a regular guest might find his refrigerator already stocked with favorite foods, or if an employee learns that someone likes stir-fry, there's likely to be a wok in

Relaxing by the swimming pool, guests can enjoy frequent cookouts and make new friends.

Each suite includes a fully equipped kitchen, allowing guests to prepare their own meals.

the kitchen by the end of the day. "A simple thing like a favorite brand of tea can make the difference between a ho-hum end to the day or coming home to something special," Lee explains.

Another amenity and a popular spot for guests is Residence Inn's Health Club, featuring Nautilus and other exercise equipment for a vigorous workout any time of day. Other recreational opportunities include a swimming pool, a heated whirlpool, and a court for basketball or tennis. As part of a program developed by Residence Inn and the American Heart Association, guests also receive information about exercises they can do in their rooms, as well as a list of "heart smart" eating tips.

Business guests will find the Residence Inn very accommodating, with its facsimile service and a meeting room for up to 30 people. And for the many international visitors the inn hosts, language courses are available through the Palmetto Association of Translators and Interpreters. Limousine service from the airport is also provided.

LEADING THE EXTENDED STAY INDUSTRY

Opened in 1985, Residence Inn Spartanburg is one of 182 properties in 41 states operated by Residence Inn by Marriott, a wholly owned subsidiary of the Marriott Corporation of Washington, D.C. The division dominates the extended-stay segment of the hospitality industry. Residence Inn properties are designed to resemble upscale residential complexes, and feature lodging accommodations that are at least 50 percent larger than traditional hotel rooms. Rates are determined by a sliding scale depending on the length of stay.

Lee emphasizes that the single most important ingredient for success at any Residence Inn is the staff. "Our employees listen for clues about how to make a stay more memorable, and they are em-

powered to do the little extras that may make a difference," she says. "We try to make sure there are a lot of 'wows,' and it's all based on finding out what people like, want, and need. We do our best to make their stay as much like home as possible."

SYMTECH Systems & Technology, Inc.

TEXTILE PRODUCTION AND FINISHING INVOLVES A COMPLEX ARRAY OF MACHINES AND equipment, each component performing a specific function interlinked with the operation of other equipment. Generally, the most efficient machines available for a process involve a number of manufacturers in different countries, doing business in different currencies and under different import/export requirements. Selection, purchase, and servicing can become quite time-consuming and involved.

SYMTECH simplifies the process for the customer. As a distributor of equipment and machinery for all segments of the textile industry, the company markets the equipment, handles installation and repair, and maintains a complete

its original size. The company's 32,000-square-foot facility faces Interstate 85 at Bryant Road.

SYMTECH has exclusive agreements to serve all of the United States and Canada for 20 equipment suppliers. It also has

turers and textile customers.

The company employs 20 service engineers, each of whom specializes in one or more product lines. SYMTECH also services the computer systems and software that drive today's textile manufacturing process. On staff are six expert electronics technicians who handle a volume of more than 3,500 repair orders on approximately 15,000 units per year.

The SYMTECH service department maintains a spare parts inventory of more than 13,000 items for nearly 100 different machines. "Since downtime is a crucial factor in the profitability of a textile operation, we stock every item that has a normal turnover, as well as the items that are vital to keeping the machines running," Balmer says.

As the representative of a wide range of textile equipment manufacturers, SYMTECH has the capability to bring together a number of suppliers to provide a complete manufacturing process. Typically SYMTECH can help a client build and maintain a complete yarn dye house, from winding and robotic loading to computer-assisted color mixing and dispensing to the dye process, radio-frequency drying, and robotic unloading and rewinding. Says Balmer, "We are interested in all opportunities to offer textile companies a more complete package in sales and servicing."

SYMTECH has enjoyed dramatic growth since its founding in 1985. Today, 70 people are employed at the company's 32,000-square-foot facility facing Interstate 85 at Bryant Road.

parts inventory. "We act as an extension of our suppliers and perform all the duties on their behalf as if they had their own subsidiaries in the United States," says Hans Balmer, president and CEO of the company.

NEARLY A DECADE OF PROSPERITY

One of the largest firms of its kind in the country serving the textile industry, SYMTECH has enjoyed dramatic growth since its founding in 1985. Sales have increased from $5 million in its first year to $40 million in 1992, and the staff has grown to 70 employees—five times

agreements with 10 suppliers to serve the northern United States. All of these companies are headquartered in Italy, Germany, Switzerland, Great Britain, or the United States.

Before Balmer started the company, most of the suppliers he now represents were established in North America and had representatives based here. In fact, Balmer came from Switzerland to the United States in 1972 as a representative for Loepfe AG. SYMTECH brought these representatives together under one roof, resulting in streamlined procedures and cost savings for the manufac-

Executive Quality Management, Inc.

COMPANIES AND CORPORATIONS HAVE A WIDE SELECTION OF QUALITY MANAGEMENT consultants to turn to these days, but very few can compare with Executive Quality Management, Inc. "We practice what we preach, so we know how difficult making changes can be in the business world," explains Joe Black, president of the management consulting firm. ◆ "For a company to become the best at what it does, each person on the payroll must make a personal decision to raise his or her level of interest, knowledge, belief, trust, and commitment. It requires true commitment by the top management to make changes, and it takes total teamwork," says George Tate, chairman and CEO of the firm.

In 1986 Joe Black and George Tate left challenging positions with Milliken & Company to found Executive Quality Management, Inc. Since then the Spartanburg firm has grown to be one of the leading continuous improvement consulting firms in the United States and has partnered with dozens of organizations—small and Fortune 500, local and international—to help those clients beat the competition.

EQM's associates, who possess professional credentials in virtually every area of business and industry, examine their customers' current structures and systems and help them build on their strengths. They also probe their clients' major problems and challenges and then custom design continuous improvement processes to address those issues. EQM's customer base ranges from manufacturing companies to a wide variety of service organizations.

A PROACTIVE APPROACH

EQM encourages a proactive approach for its clients. The founders believe that a company must commit to a "preventive" rather than a "firefighter" mentality if quality and customer service improvements are to last. They also emphasize the partnership aspect of EQM's relationship with clients. "Our largest differential advantage in the marketplace is the caliber of associates who have chosen to work with our company and the relationships they forge with our customers," says Tate.

EQM has built its process around a set of basic principles that individuals within an organization can apply to both their professional and personal lives. "At EQM, quality is more than a product or service; it is everything we do," says Black. "Many quality improvement procedures being taught and used today focus too heavily on technology. Our experience tells us that people are the key to quality. Without commitment from every associate on a company's payroll, excellent quality and service simply will not happen."

EQM sees the '90s as a transition decade in the United States relative to changes in corporate structure and management philosophies. "There are incredible opportunities for companies to develop a dynamic, customer-centered culture for long-term stability and growth," says Black. "It's an exciting time to be in business, especially if you know how to tap the human potential."

Chairman and CEO George Tate and President Joe Black founded EQM in 1986.

145

Blockbuster Entertainment Corporation

I N SIX SHORT YEARS, A GROUP OF BLOCKBUSTER VIDEO FRANCHISE OWNERS HAVE HELPED redefine the standards of the home entertainment industry and are placing a trademark of friendly, family fun on a success story still in the making. ◆ WJB Video, a limited partnership, intended to open just three Blockbuster stores when it began in Spartanburg in 1987. But by the end of 1993, the partnership had grown to include 210 stores employing 4,000 people from Virginia to Florida. At that time, the franchise stores were

Under the innovative KIDPRINT program (right), children are videotaped, along with important personal information, for use by law enforcement agencies should the child become lost.

Blockbuster's Southeastern Zone Office (right) is located on East Main Street in Spartanburg.

absorbed into parent company Blockbuster Entertainment Corporation, and one of the investors, George Dean Johnson Jr., was named president of its Domestic Consumer Division in Fort Lauderdale, Florida. Spartanburg is now home to the Southeastern Zone Office, which is continuing Blockbuster's regional success and participating in development of the corporation's newest products— Discovery Zone indoor playgrounds, Blockbuster Music Plus stores, and Blockbuster video game centers.

FRIENDLY, FAMILY ORIENTATION

From the bright and orderly appearance of the stores to personalized service, WJB Video has strived to convey a sense of family values, enhanced by extensive employee training and attention to detail. Today, employees are empowered to provide an unmatched level of customer service by adhering to four basic principles: "Treat each customer as your guest; treat fellow employees as you want to be treated; be a good steward of all that is entrusted to you; and use good judgment at all times."

Blockbuster's innovative spirit provided the platform for success in Spartanburg. It was the first company to offer three evenings of viewing at one price and the first to

display videos on the shelves to expedite choices. It also instituted flexible hours, drop boxes for convenient returns, and a standard selection of 10,000 or more titles per store, including a large kids' collection and only tasteful adult fare. A toll-free customer response number was prominently displayed at all locations.

Today, when customers enter a Blockbuster store, they are greeted with an offer of assistance. Children are drawn to a kids' corner where they are entertained by videos playing continuously, allowing parents to browse. The stock is clearly organized and marked, with new releases lining a prominent wall. Once selections are made, customers are thanked by name at the checkout counter.

The stores have become part of their communities, offering such innovative services as KIDPRINT. Under this program, children are videotaped, along with important personal information, for use by law enforcement agencies should the child become lost. More than 300,000 children participated in KIDPRINT in 1993 alone. The stores also strive to cater their video selection to community tastes, and a section of no-fee rentals is available on subjects ranging from parenting skills to drug and alcohol abuse.

As Blockbuster Entertainment continues to develop new products and services, the concepts that made WJB Video successful are now being employed at the corporate level, where George Dean Johnson Jr. leads a total of 2,600 video stores. The Spartanburg office, with its 115 employees, will continue to play a pivotal role in the ongoing Blockbuster success story as the recognized leader in the video rental industry.

Drennan, Shelor, Cole & Evins, P.A.

DRENNAN, SHELOR, COLE & EVINS, P.A. WAS FOUNDED IN 1987 BY FOUR FORMER members of one of Spartanburg's largest law firms. The firm's guiding philosophy is that the contemporary legal requirements of its clients must be tempered by the long view of those needs, according to James B. Drennan III, one of the firm's shareholders. ◆ The firm provides a broad range of legal services, and its members have special expertise in estate planning, probate, business and commercial

matters, and litigation. The firm's success in meeting this basic goal is reflected in the variety of interests to which its four attorneys provide counsel. Among its clients are not only individuals but public utilities, insurance companies, domestic and international manufacturing concerns, product distributors, shopping centers, development groups, and real estate developers. As general U.S. counsel for a worldwide textile equipment group and South Carolina counsel for a large petroleum pipeline transmission company, among other such relationships, the firm has demonstrated its ability to meet the long-term needs of its clients, both large and small.

THE PRINCIPALS

The firm's four attorneys are graduates of the University of South Carolina School of Law and have 84 years of cumulative experience in the practice of law. Located in a historic building in downtown Spartanburg, the firm's offices provide a quiet, dignified setting that is comfortable for client and lawyer alike.

James B. Drennan III is a certified specialist in estate planning and probate law in South Carolina. A Fellow of the American College of Trust and Estate Counsel, he chaired the committee of the South Carolina Bar that drafted the current South Carolina Probate Code. His expertise has been further recognized by his inclusion in *The Best Lawyers in America*, a publication comprising less than 1 percent of attorneys in the United States. Drennan also has extensive experience in business and corporate affairs, as well as litigation related

to his areas of expertise.

Robert A. Shelor emphasizes corporate, business, and real estate matters in his practice. He holds an undergraduate degree from Stanford University and a bachelor's degree from the American Institute for Foreign Trade in Phoenix, Arizona. Shelor has served as a member of the House of Delegates of the South Carolina Bar Association.

Edward R. Cole devotes the majority of his practice to a wide range of litigated matters, including business and corporate affairs, product liability, and insurance-related concerns. He also serves as United States general counsel for a worldwide manufacturing concern and as state counsel for a regional petroleum pipeline company. Cole is a member of the South Carolina Defense Trial Attorneys' Association, the Defense Research Institute, and the Judicial Conference of the United States Fourth Circuit Court of Appeals. He received his undergraduate degree from Wofford College in Spartanburg.

T. Alexander Evins limits his practice primarily to corporate business and commercial matters. Since 1990 he has served as general counsel to the Spartanburg Area Chamber of Commerce. A lifelong resident of Spartanburg, Evins received his undergraduate degree from the University of Georgia.

"All of us are strongly committed to the highest principles and business ethics," says Drennan, "and our clients are like-minded. Success to us is growing in terms of legal acumen and quality client service, while maintaining our reputation for integrity and fairness."

SERVING THE COMMUNITY

Dedicated not only to providing high-quality representation for its clients, the firm is also committed to making Spartanburg a better community for all citizens. Says Drennan, "The Spartanburg community is blessed with the strength it derives from many volunteer efforts. Drennan, Shelor, Cole & Evins strives to give back some of the benefits we derive from being a part of the community."

As evidence of this commitment, firm members serve on the boards of hospital foundations and civic and social organizations. They are active in the Arts Council of Spartanburg County, the Spartanburg County Historical Society, the Spartanburg YMCA, and the Spartanburg Little Theatre, among others. Two members of the firm are graduates of Leadership Spartanburg, and one member now serves as an advisor to that program and to Junior Leadership Spartanburg, both sponsored by the Spartanburg Area Chamber of Commerce to encourage the development of community leaders.

The firm's shareholders are (from left to right) Bob Shelor, Jim Drennan, Ed Cole, and Alex Evins.

Somet of America, Inc.

SOMET OF AMERICA, INC. IS THE MARKETING AND SERVICE ARM OF BERGAMO, ITALY-BASED Somet SpA, the world's largest producer of rapier weaving machines. Somet technology is renowned worldwide for the quality production of woven fabrics, including complex Jacquard fabrics in which designs are woven into the fabric as opposed to being printed. These fabrics are widely utilized in domestic and automotive upholstery, high-fashion apparel, neckties, and many other products.

Somet equipment is in use throughout North America, including the Reeves Brothers, Inc. Chesnee Division in Chesnee, South Carolina (below left), and Valdese Weavers, Inc. in Valdese, North Carolina (below right).

From its Spartanburg facility at the intersection of I-85 and I-26 (bottom), Somet of America, Inc. provides sales, technical support, spare parts, and training for its versatile weaving equipment.

Somet opened its U.S. operation in Spartanburg in 1987 to better serve the North American market. "At that time, our market share was insignificant," says General Manager K.G. Melling, of Somet of America, Inc., "but today we are a leading supplier of rapier weaving machines in the United States, which is the world's second largest end-user of the Somet THEMA Rapier Weaving Machine."

In 1992 Somet SpA celebrated its 25th anniversary and the installation of its 40,000th machine. Young for a textile machinery manufacturer but sophisticated by any standards, Somet reached several other milestones in 1992: the introduction of the state-of-the-art THEMA 11E Rapier Weaving Machine; the launching of a new air jet weaving machine, the STAR 15; and the receipt of the Certification of Quality in accordance with the European UNI EN 29000 and

29001 standards. These standards are periodically verified and are used universally to guarantee quality at all levels of manufacturing.

THE ADVANTAGES OF SOMET EQUIPMENT

From its attractive Spartanburg facility, located at the intersection of I-85 and I-26, Somet of America, Inc. provides sales, technical support, spare parts, and training for its weaving equipment used to produce many types of fabric, from fine silk to heavy industrial fabrics.

"Key features of our equipment include versatility, productivity, fabric quality, and user-friendli-

ness," K.G. Melling says. "For our U.S. customers, our technology helps in maintaining the competitive edge against imports." The Somet Weaving System enables the user to develop new and specialized fabrics that can be produced on existing equipment.

Leading edge technology is a significant factor. For example, Somet assisted a North Carolina plant in becoming the first Jacquard weaving operation in the world to be totally computerized. Somet rapier weaving machines are equipped with electronics that allow bidirectional communication with a host computer. Such operations as pattern changes, scheduling, and process control are all accomplished through computerization. The system is so sophisticated that the plant is able to make an average of 180 pattern changes per day, using more than 30,000 style combinations. Human involvement has been minimized and efficiency increased.

This level of success has been made possible by the on-board SOCOS computing system, which monitors and controls machine status. The system is also used to set machine and fabric parameters. This and other technological advances place Somet high in customer ratings and end-user satisfaction.

"With our people, the innovation we bring to the market, and our ability to produce cost-effective weaving equipment," concludes K.G. Melling, "we have a very bright future."

Harry's on Morgan Square

O N ANY GIVEN NIGHT, YOU CAN FIND JUST ABOUT ANYONE AT HARRY'S ON MORGAN Square—prospective new businesses discussing a Spartanburg location with chamber of commerce officials, a Converse College student taking her dad out to dinner, or a group of Wofford College professors gathering for a pint of Bass Pale Ale and a tall tale. Since it opened in July 1988, Harry's has become a standard in Spartanburg when people agree to "do lunch" or "go somewhere special for dinner."

Named for co-owner Harry Stathakis, the restaurant has grown to fit its name, according to Harry's brother and business partner Terry Stathakis. "I used to live in New York, where Harry's just south of Wall Street is known for its quality," he says. "Harry's Bar in Venice was a frequent hangout for Ernest Hemingway and his pals. The Harry's New York Bar in Paris has a history that includes Henry Capriani, and I hear that's where drinks were first called cocktails."

Living up to its distinguished name, Harry's on Morgan Square has offered high-quality New York-style dining and a popular continental menu since it opened—to the skepticism of some. "We were actually ahead of our time. We made the decision to open the restaurant downtown, where things looked pretty bad before TW Services (now Flagstar) built a high-rise and moved hundreds of white-collar employees down here," Stathakis recalls. "We were pioneers."

Despite the risk, the brothers were determined to make the restaurant work. To save money, Terry and his wife lived in an apartment above the restaurant for the first year. Likewise, the City of Spartanburg helped the founders locate tax credits and interest subsidies for renovating a building in the historic district.

BUILDING A REPUTATION

According to Stathakis, people come to Harry's for the service, the atmosphere, and the food—in that order. If Harry's has a "signature"

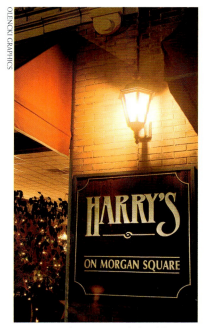

item, it is the seasoned, freshly cooked potato chips served at lunchtime. The evening menu includes lamb, pastas, veal, seafood, and beef, as well as a full complement of appetizers, soups, salads, and desserts—including mousse pies, carrot cake, and New York-style cheesecake. Harry's also offers an excellent selection of fine wines.

Employing 30 people, the restaurant now includes a banquet room upstairs. Since it opened in 1989, the banquet facility has been a favorite among area businesses and colleges for special events and for holiday parties. Harry's has hosted bar mitzvahs, a number of pre-dance dinners, and cast parties for touring Broadway shows appearing at Spartanburg Memorial Auditorium.

Harry's is also gaining a regional reputation. Recently, a company based in nearby Greenville booked the restaurant for its Christmas party. And Harry's was the first Spartanburg restaurant ever invited to participate in Greenville's March of Dimes Chef's Auction.

While Terry Stathakis admits the restaurant business means long hours and hard work, he credits the venture's success to an ability to listen to customers and adapt to their needs—and to Harry, who

oversees the chef and the kitchen operations.

When asked what the future holds for Harry's on Morgan Square, Stathakis says, grinning, "An expensive cappuccino machine."

Located in downtown Spartanburg, Harry's on Morgan Square has built a solid reputation for its excellent service, atmosphere, and food.

Edwards, Ballard, Bishop, Sturm, Clark and Keim, P.A.

EDWARDS, BALLARD, BISHOP, STURM, CLARK AND KEIM, P.A., HAS BUILT A CLIENT BASE of more than 350 companies, representing management exclusively in all aspects of employment, labor, environmental, workplace safety and health, workers' compensation, and employee benefits law. The firm also provides counseling in legislative affairs and handles immigration matters for numerous Upstate businesses. Among its clients are companies in the Spartanburg area and throughout the Southeast,

including a growing number of businesses in North Carolina, served through an office in Winston-Salem. The firm's clients range from regional operations, such as hospitals, to multinational corporations.

A UNIQUE FOCUS

Recently, Edwards, Ballard, Bishop, Sturm, Clark and Keim, P.A., has

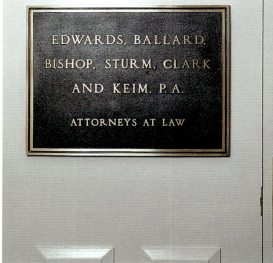

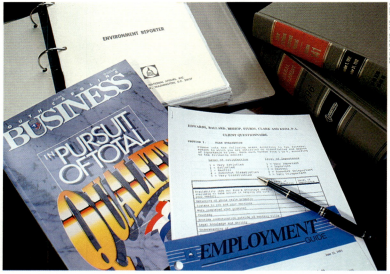

Serving a client base of more than 350 companies, the firm represents management in all aspects of employment, labor, environmental, workplace safety and health, workers' compensation, and employee benefits law.

refined its focus with the goal of improving client services through Total Quality Management (TQM). "Historically, law firms have defined for themselves what quality is—how a case is to be handled, the time spent with the client, how many lawyers will be involved," explains James F. Edwards Jr., a partner in the firm. "With TQM, we have a formal system that will consistently meet or exceed our clients' needs."

Edwards, Ballard, Bishop, Sturm, Clark and Keim, P.A., is one of the first law firms in the Southeast to truly adopt the principles of TQM, a quality improvement pro-

cess in use by manufacturers worldwide and now being practiced by foresighted service providers, such as banks, insurance companies, and charitable organizations. "TQM places a strong emphasis on the client—helping us find out on a regular basis what they think and continuously improving our response to those needs through employee involvement," Edwards says.

PRACTICING PREVENTIVE LAW

In addition to its array of traditional legal services, the firm conducts intensive training programs to help companies avoid adverse situations. Training sessions cover such topics as union avoidance, substance abuse prevention, employee benefits practices, and safety and health issues. As laws and their enforcement change, the firm encourages clients to update their knowledge of equal employment, age discrimination, affirmative action, and disability laws. "In our practice areas, if you don't emphasize preventive law, you're

headed for trouble," says Edwards.

Firm members believe that the most critical factor affecting the growth and prosperity of employers in the '90s and into the 21st century is human resources. Therefore, the development and proper management of an employer's work force has never been more important. Edwards, Ballard, Bishop, Sturm, Clark and Keim, P.A., is dedicated to working in an efficient and cost-effective manner to help management prevent unwanted legal entanglements before they occur and handle conflicts that cannot be avoided. "Our number one priority is to assist managers in their efforts to operate productively and profitably," the partners say.

Adds Edwards, "We want our clients to be around for many tomorrows, and to be certain that happens, we have to make sure we're giving them our best. Along with our practicing preventive law, TQM has given us the right tools to do just that."

150

LTG Technologies, Inc.

LTG TECHNOLOGIES, INC. OPENED IN SPARTANBURG IN 1990 WITH HELMUT STUEBLE AS its only employee. In just three years, the company, the only U.S. subsidiary of LTG Lufttechnische GmbH of Stuttgart, Germany, has grown to 25 employees, with plans to expand in the near future. Stueble is president of the company, which has offices facing Interstate 85 in Spartanburg. ◆ Two of the four divisions of the Stuttgart company are represented by the U.S. subsidiary. One involves the manufacture

of components and the engineering, installation, and marketing of air-conditioning, filtration, and waste handling systems for the textile industry. With its advanced equipment and design capabilities, LTG is helping to meet the increasingly stricter regulations for air quality and temperature control in yarn spinning, weaving, and fiber processing.

The second and also growing company division designs, manufactures, and installs drying ovens and pollution control equipment for the metal packaging and printing industry. The ovens are used primarily to cure coated or printed metal sheets that will eventually be used to make cans for packaging products such as food and beverages. All drying ovens can be equipped with integrated oxidizers for the removal of solvent fumes; retrofitting of older ovens is becoming increasingly popular. The LTG drying technology is well advanced to meet the requirements of the EPA, as well as the expectations of American clients.

According to Stueble, LTG's strengths are its engineering capabilities, its quality components, and its willingness to work closely with clients to custom-design systems. "We sell nothing as a shelf item," says Stueble. "Each system is engineered and designed to meet a specific need in a certain application."

Among the company's major U.S. customers are Avondale Mills, Inman Mills, Mayfair Mills, Milliken & Company, Russell Corporation, Sara Lee Knit Products, and Westpoint Pepperell for the textile division, and Crown Cork & Seal, Finger Lakes Packaging, and

Independent Can Company for the drying division.

IN THE FOREFRONT OF AIR-HANDLING TECHNOLOGY

LTG Lufttechnische GmbH, now in its third generation of same-family ownership, was founded in 1924 by Dr. Albert Klein. The first company in Germany to specialize in air-handling technology, LTG

today engineers and manufactures equipment for a wide range of industrial and commercial applications. The company employs 1,200 people, including seven branch offices in Germany and seven subsidiaries in Austria, France, Germany, Hong Kong, Italy, Singapore, and the United States.

LTG Technologies' choice of Spartanburg for its first U.S. location was based on three primary factors, Stueble says. The first was simple geography: Spartanburg is

at the center of the country's textile industry. The second factor was the administrative and sales support offered by SYMTECH Systems & Technologies, with which LTG shares a building. The third consideration was the community. Stueble comments, "People are friendly and open-minded in Spartanburg, and that is important to us."

Stueble predicts rapid growth for the company as it continues to successfully market its products and as clients realize the productivity and environmental enhancements possible through LTG's efficient systems. "We are happy with our Spartanburg operations and plan to stay," he says. "We see many opportunities here with an optimistic and forward-thinking textile industry as well as the innovative can-making industry."

Since LTG Technologies opened in Spartanburg in 1990, President Helmut Stueble (left) has seen the company grow to 25 employees, with plans to expand in the near future.

The company's strengths are its engineering capabilities (above), its quality components, and its willingness to work closely with clients to custom-design systems.

BMW Manufacturing Corp.

BMW HAS A STRAIGHTFORWARD GOAL FOR ITS NEW SPARTANBURG COUNTY OPERATION: to see that BMWs manufactured in South Carolina are famous around the world. "BMW will build cars here not just for the American market, but to export superior quality automobiles to each of the 100-plus countries where our autos are sold," says Al Kinzer, president of BMW Manufacturing Corp. ◆ The German company is the first luxury automaker to invest in a U.S. facility to build cars for worldwide

sales. Construction of the new production facility, located near the Greenville-Spartanburg Airport, began in April 1993, with the first cars scheduled to roll off the assembly line in the late fall of 1994. The plant, which has the potential

jacket uniform that will make the operation look more like a research laboratory than a typical assembly plant. The uniform choice reflects the company's philosophy that each individual contributes to its success. Says Kinzer, "We are de-

second largest market behind its home country of Germany.

Among the reasons BMW chose South Carolina are the area's interstate highway system, which provides easy access to major markets in all directions, and the deep-

Construction of BMW's new production facility (right), located near the Greenville-Spartanburg Airport, began in 1993, with the first cars scheduled to roll off the assembly line in the late fall of 1994.

Groundbreaking ceremonies were held on September 30, 1992 (above).

to produce up to 90,000 cars annually, will increase gradually from its initial employment of 1,200 individuals to 2,000 production associates by the end of the decade.

The 1.2 million-square-foot operation is intended to be a "flexible" automobile plant. Combining new technologies with highly skilled workmanship, it will be able to produce several different models from the same assembly line, depending on demand. The plant is designed to allow cars to be assembled in a linear process under one roof for maximum efficiency.

Further contributing to the "flexible" atmosphere, all associates are on a first-name basis, and the company has adopted a white-

termined to operate on a system of oneness and equality."

WHY SPARTANBURG?

BMW chose the United States for its newest production facility for three primary reasons. First of all, the company has total confidence in the ability of American workers to produce BMW automobiles of world-class quality. Secondly, a U.S. operation will broaden BMW's international competitive base by exporting at least 50 percent of the company's overall production, thus reducing its dependence on one currency. Finally, the new facility will help fulfill a company goal to strengthen its long-term commitment to the United States, BMW's

water port of Charleston, which will be an import area for autos and parts, as well as a platform for exporting the automobiles assembled locally. The Greenville-Spartanburg Airport will allow BMW to bring in key components for just-in-time production.

Another factor in the decision and the success of the company is the assistance provided by South Carolina's technical training program. South Carolina Job Service will provide initial screening of applicants, then the Special Schools Program of the State Board of Technical and Comprehensive Education will train BMW's new associates at no cost to the company. The program meets BMW's

In 1991 the company introduced its Model 3 series, the first automobile designed to be recyclable. More than 80 percent of the car by weight may be recycled at three authorized centers in the United States.

With its distinctive line of luxury automobiles (left), BMW remains one of the world's best-known automakers.

needs to develop the skills necessary to build high-quality products.

"We have often been reminded of the risks associated with the production of German cars in another country," said Chairman Emeritus Eberhard von Kuenheim at the groundbreaking ceremony on September 30, 1992. "There are two sides to quality: the technical side and the human side. The combination of people in South Carolina and BMW will cover both."

SHOWCASING BMW INNOVATION

Company officials say quality and innovation will be the hallmarks of the new operation. In the past, BMW has led the world's auto manufacturers in such cutting-edge innovations as the electronic fuel injection system, anti-lock brakes, and the first automobiles produced without ozone-damaging chlorofluorocarbons (CFCs). In 1991 the company introduced its Model 3 series, the first automobile designed to be recyclable. More than 80 percent of the car by weight may be recycled at three authorized centers in the United States. BMW is also investigating the production feasibility of emission-free automobiles such as the electric car.

These and other highlights of the company and its cars will be showcased at a communications center within the Spartanburg facility, where up to 50,000 visitors and BMW enthusiasts are expected to visit each year. The center is designed to be educational, fun, and interactive, offering greater understanding of the automobile and the company. The center will also host symposia on topics such as the environment, safety, and new technologies.

The vision of BMW Manufacturing Corp. is to be an example for leading-edge concepts not just in technology but also in how the company conducts business. Since the early stages of plant design, its minority business involvement initiative has drawn interest from throughout the region. "We continually ask ourselves, 'What would a leader do in this situation?' We must consider ourselves a role model and approach every opportunity from the viewpoint of its long-range effect on our many communities and our industry," Kinzer says.

In welcoming BMW to Spartanburg and Upstate South Carolina at the groundbreaking, Governor Carroll Campbell acknowledged the company's new role: "Community life, the environment, building a future for our children . . . these are issues we care about in South Carolina, and these are issues BMW cares about as a corporate citizen. We share your vision."

Helima Helvetion International

I N JUST FIVE YEARS, HELIMA HELVETION INTERNATIONAL'S U.S. PRESENCE HAS GROWN FROM A small sales and distribution office in New York to a thriving, 120,000-square-foot manufacturing operation in Spartanburg County. ◆ The company manufactures and sells window spacer bars, which are rolled and formed aluminum bars used to hold glass window panes in place. Helima also produces highly customized aluminum tubing for the worldwide automotive industry, including heat exchangers, water coolers, charge air

coolers, oil coolers, and air conditioning tubing made of core alloys and claddings designed to meet customers' individual requirements and market demand.

"We started in 1988 with a U.S. sales and distribution office in New York. By 1991 it had become too difficult to import all of the material we needed," says Willy Ruefenacht, president of Helima's

U.S. operation located in Duncan, just east of Spartanburg. Because a growing number of customers were buying sizable quantities of Helima's products, it became imperative to establish a manufacturing center in the United States.

Ruefenacht toured the country looking at potential sites for the operation, including the 100-acre Spartangreen Business Park in

Duncan. He was drawn by the availability of an attractive building facing Interstate 85, along with the distribution capabilities of the Port of Charleston and the Greenville-Spartanburg Airport.

The most important enticement, however, was South Carolina's outstanding technical training system. During the facility's start-up period, the Special

Helima Helvetion's 120,000-square-foot facility houses machine, tooling, and electronics shops, as well as administrative offices and a manufacturing area.

STEPHEN STINSON

BLAKE PRAYTOR

The company produces highly customized aluminum tubing for the worldwide automotive industry, including heat exchangers, water coolers, charge air coolers, oil coolers, and air conditioning tubing.

Schools Division of the State Board for Comprehensive and Technical Education, in conjunction with the South Carolina Job Service, provided free training to potential Helima employees and even sent a team to Germany to undergo eight months of technical training. "I cannot stress how valuable this kind of support is to a start-up company. The South Carolina Job Service recruits the right people, then helps them learn your business through a customized training program," Ruefenacht explains. "We accepted 90 percent of the people who attended the first two schools."

The program was such a success that Helima was among a

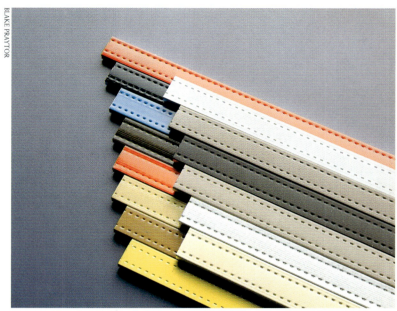

select group of companies featured recently in an NBC news story about South Carolina's Special Schools program. Several of Helima's employees were interviewed about their positive experiences in the innovative training initiative.

The Spartanburg Area Chamber of Commerce and the State Development Board provided the company additional assistance with site selection and transition. "They were so helpful and made it so much easier from the moment we met," says Ruefenacht. "They even helped with the grand opening ceremonies."

A UNIQUE MANUFACTURING FACILITY

During the eight-month training period before production began, Helima's U.S. headquarters was finished to company specifications, including the addition of a fountain in the foyer and a curved stairway leading to beautifully appointed second-floor offices and a spacious conference room. The facility houses machine, tooling, and electronics shops, as well as administrative offices and a manufacturing area.

"We bought the building in December 1991 and had our grand

opening in October 1992. In that time period we even built all of our manufacturing machines in-house to maintain security," explains Ruefenacht. "No one actually believed we could do it in a few short months. It was a tremendous achievement for our people."

A GROWING CLIENT BASE

With its growing success in the United States as a foundation, Helima in its first year of operation has expanded its client base to serve markets in Canada, Mexico, Venezuela, Chile, Brazil, and Australia. The company also is beginning to export some of its production back to Europe through a license and technology transfer agreement with The Lingemann Group, which is headquartered in Wuppertal, Germany. But despite Helima's growth in the global market, Ruefenacht says that the Spartanburg County operation is "an American company."

Helima's 72 local employees include toolmakers, welders, metalworking professionals, electronic engineers, electricians, and machine operators, as well as office and warehouse staff. The company expects to employ more than 100 people by 1994 and as many as 400 by 1998.

"We think our market will grow immensely in coming years," Ruefenacht says, pointing out that more than 85 percent of truck radiators currently are made of relatively heavy copper and brass. As higher taxes and fuel prices drive the automotive industry toward more lightweight materials, Helima Helvetion International is poised to fill an emerging market niche. "Our aluminum tubes are lightweight, fuel-saving, and long-lasting," adds Ruefenacht. "As a result, our growth could be explosive."

In order to continue meeting market demands for its quality products, Helima has embraced ISO 9000 standards and methods, the most stringent in industry today. Helima also recently purchased the 15 acres surrounding its building to accommodate future expansions.

A native of Lucerne, Switzerland, Willy Ruefenacht has found Spartanburg County to be an excellent business location and a great place to call home. "The American community is an interesting and friendly aspect of the area," Ruefenacht says. "For me, Spartanburg County is now home."

The company manufactures and sells window spacer bars, which are rolled and formed aluminum bars used to hold glass window panes in place.

Wilson World Hotel

A MID THE KEEN COMPETITION OF SPARTANBURG'S HOSPITALITY INDUSTRY, ATTITUDE CAN make all the difference. At the Wilson World Hotel on Fairforest Road near the intersection of I-26 and I-85, the attitude clearly projected to guests is, "Let me take care of that for you." ◆ "We are a full-service and service-driven hotel," says Paul Kelley, general manager of the hotel, which is conveniently located near medical centers, colleges, and many businesses. "We have free transportation to the air-

port, and we are the only hotel with a bellman. When a guest tells any staff member about a need, we do all we can to meet it."

The emphasis on superior service is a priority of the hotel's owners—Kemmons Wilson Sr., founder of Holiday Inns, and Frederick Dent Sr., chairman of Mayfair Mills, a textile company headquartered in Spartanburg. Wilson, after selling his Holiday Inns interests in the 1970s, turned his attention to developing fine but affordable hotel properties. Eighteen Wilson World Hotels and Wilson Inns properties have opened in eight Southeastern states since 1984. Spartanburg's Wilson World opened in April 1990 as a joint venture of Wilson and Dent.

OUTSTANDING SERVICE AND AMENITIES

The first indication that guests are in for a special stay is the bellman who greets them at the door. "If you need theater or ball game tickets, if you want to know where to play a round of golf, or if a group wants to go shopping, the bellman can help arrange those activities," says Kelley. "Our bellmen are perceptive and attentive. They realize they make the difference in our level of service."

The hotel is attractively designed around a five-story enclosed atrium featuring a pool and restaurant, with room balconies overlooking. All of the hotel's 200 rooms are oversized, with king- or double king-size beds and refrigerators. Ninety of the rooms are suites—furnished with microwave

ovens, hair dryers, refrigerators, and wet bars—and are suitable for long-term stays. The hotel also features a game room and a fully equipped exercise room.

With more than 13,000 square feet of meeting space in 13 rooms, Wilson World hosts numerous seminars and meetings ranging in size from 10 to 300 people. Wedding receptions, reunions, and

group meetings grace its halls regularly. Meeting services may include catering for meals and breaks, as well as developing spouse activity plans.

EXPECT A PLEASANT STAY

Weekday evenings feature "Hungry Hour" in the atrium, where a 12-foot table is laden with snack foods to accompany cocktails. International specialties, seafood, and

"Food For Your Fingers" are some of the fare offered.

For meals in a casual atmosphere, the hotel's Blue Ridge Cafe offers a full menu, as well as a soup and salad bar, breakfast and lunch buffets, and a "build your own sundae" bar. The restaurant's offerings meet the needs of the health-conscious or diet-restricted traveler, but also tempt sophisti-

cated palates with special dishes.

Every evening, melodies waft through the hotel from the white grand piano in the atrium lobby, creating an ambience of serenity and elegance. In Spartanburg, it's no surprise that the Wilson World Hotel has become a favorite among business travelers, as well as families, because of its spacious, comfortable atmosphere.

The Wilson World Hotel is designed around an attractive, five-story enclosed atrium featuring a pool and restaurant, with room balconies overlooking.

OLENCKI GRAPHICS

Photographers

Michael Corbin is a teacher of art and photography at Carver Junior High School in Spartanburg School District Seven. A graduate of the University of Cincinnati, with a master's degree from Converse College, he specializes in black-and-white, fine art photography. Corbin's photography curriculum for the school district has won numerous awards and grants. His images have been featured in five exhibits throughout South Carolina since 1992.

Steve Fincher established Steve Fincher Photography, specializing in commercial photography, in 1982. His work in fashion photography has been published in *Redbook*, *Women's Wear Daily*, *Teen*, and *Seventeen*. Fincher's corporate clients include adidas, Beverage Air, BMW, Lockwood Greene, and Milliken & Company. His 8,000-square-foot studio in Spartanburg contains a full-color processing and printing lab, as well as an electronic imaging system.

John C. Gillespie, a native of Spartanburg, is a graphic artist with KEMET Electronics in Greenville, South Carolina. A graduate of Central Wesleyan College, Gillespie formerly worked as an audio-visual specialist at Spartanburg Regional Medical Center and spent several years as a free-lance photographer. His awards include Best New Artist of Show in 1983 at the Spartanburg Art Center and First Place in the 1990 Converse College Art Show.

Robert L. Gregory III, a lifelong resident of Spartanburg, is a commercial photographer employed by Steve Fincher Photography. Gregory's work has been published in the *Spartanburg Herald Journal*, and his awards include recognition in 1993 from the South Carolina Professional Photographers Association.

James Huff, a native of Spartanburg, is a photographer and graphic artist with Olencki Graphics. He was one of three photographers whose work was exhibited in the first all-photography show at the Spartanburg Art Center Gallery in 1985. In the 1970s, he specialized in motor-sports photography, and his work appeared in numerous national publications, including Petersen's *Motorcyclist*, *Cycle*, and *Popular Science*. Huff also teaches courses in stained glass at the Art Center.

Diana Anderson Olencki is an art teacher at Fairforest Middle School in Spartanburg. A graduate of the master's program at the University of South Carolina and a former photography student at the Rhode Island School of Design, Olencki specializes in black-and-white photography. She has received recognition in numerous photography competitions, including those of Spartanburg's Spring Fling, the South Carolina Association of School Public Relations, and Kodak's Cameras in the Curriculum project.

Andrew Parker is a free-lance photographer specializing in editorial and promotional photography and individual commissions. A native of Spartanburg and graduate of Clemson University, he began his career in fashion, and formerly assisted New York-based fashion/fine art photographer Bruce Weber. Parker's work has been featured in various group and individual exhibits.

Stephen Stinson studied photography at The Art Institute of Atlanta and founded Stephen Stinson Photography in Spartanburg in 1993. He specializes in commercial photography for clients in Upstate South Carolina and western North Carolina. Stinson's work has been seen throughout the community in several solo exhibits.

Clay Terrell and his wife, **Barbara**, are owners of Terrell Photography, a 30-year-old business established by Clay's father, the late Marvin C. Terrell, Jr. A Spartanburg native and a professional photographer for more than 18 years, Clay Terrell specializes in portrait and wedding photography in the studio and on location.

Index to Patrons